The Effective Team's Operational Excellence Workbook

By Elisabeth Goodman

RiverRhee Publishing

Published in the United Kingdom by RiverRhee Publishing, a trading name of RiverRhee Consulting Ltd, 49 Meldreth Road, Shepreth, Nr Royston, Herts SG8 6PS.

Copyright © Elisabeth Goodman 2015

All rights reserved. No portion of this book may be reproduced, stored in a retrieval system or transmitted at any time or by any means mechanical, electronic, photocopying, recording or otherwise, without prior written permission of the publisher.

The right of Elisabeth Goodman to be identified as the author of this work has been asserted by her in accordance with the Copyright, Designs and Patent Act, 1988.

A CIP record of this book is available from the British Library.

First printed in June 2015.

ISBN 978-0-9926323-7-3

Printed in Great Britain by Cambridge Printers Limited

Contents

Acknowledgements	i
Preface	ii
Introduction to the Practical Scenarios	iii
Chapter 1 The Context for your Journey	1
Chapter 2 Working with your Customers	7
Chapter 3 Gathering Data	17
Chapter 4 Treating the Root Cause	27
Chapter 5 Exploring Solutions	39
Chapter 6 What Happens Next?	47
Why Six Sigma?	50
Full Page Versions of Materials for Use in Workshops	53
Further Reading	61

Acknowledgements

My journey into operational excellence began in the 1990s, when I was working at SmithKline Beecham and Ian Hau coached us on the many principles and tools that shaped 'The Simply Better Way'. Our Senior VP, Ford Calhoun, encouraged us to "find those hidden treasures": those problems that would help us to reduce fire fighting and proactively improve our day-to-day processes and projects. My then manager, Wayne Faulkner, gave us the time and resources to explore 'Total Quality Management' and to create 'Quality Circles' with people engaged in similar work. This approach had the added benefits of building strong relationships across our globally dispersed teams and opportunities to learn about and share good practices.

It is thanks to these early advocates that continuous improvement became an integral part of my way of working. This mindset and approach was kindled anew in the early 2000s when Sue Parkins championed the adoption of Lean and Six Sigma within R&D at GlaxoSmithKline. With Sue's teaching I became part of the team in 2005-2006 that rolled out 'R&D Enhance' at GSK. Other members of that team were Nigel Clark, Craig Lehoullier, Margie Gardiner and Gary Aldam.

The principles and tools that I learnt at GSK form the basis of what my Associate John Riddell and I have adapted and now use in our work with managers and teams in Library and Information Management, in the Life Sciences and in SMEs (Small and Medium Enterprises), and indeed in all organisations and in all sectors and disciplines where there are opportunities for achieving and maintaining operational excellence.

This is the third of my workbooks for effective teams. My thanks go to Nathaniel Spain again for conceiving and creating the book cover illustration, and for his skillful rendering of the various other drawings that appear in this book as well as in my courses and blogs. Isabelle Spain has helped me to create some compelling chapter headings. Jonathan Spain continues to be my greatest fan and enthusiastic co-author for the RiverRhee Publishing brand. Thank you.

Preface

I work with a lot of managers and teams who care passionately about their work and yet feel frustrated about the lack of time and resources that they have to do it well. They often feel overwhelmed by the sheer volume of what they have to do, by the amount of mundane and repetitive work, and by the lack of time available for planning ahead, reaching out to customers, and for personal and professional development.

Operational excellence is about having the necessary tools and capabilities, and making the time to pay attention to why we do what we do in our work, and how we go about it. It enables us to focus on what is important to our customers, do less fire fighting, and spend more time being visionary and innovative. It creates a more fulfilling work environment where everyone knows their role and actively contributes to the effective achievement of the organisation's goals and the efficient flow of its end-to-end processes.

I have coached and facilitated many individuals and teams in their adoption of operational excellence principles and tools (based on Lean and Six Sigma – more on this later). We have a lot of fun using tools such as the '5 Why's' to explore all the possible root causes for sometimes painful issues that people have been encountering in their day-to-day work. It never ceases to give me a 'buzz' as the people I work with realise that there are solutions within their reach to tackle these problems, and convincing data with which to influence their managers and colleagues.

Operational excellence not only gives managers and teams the principles, tools and capabilities to continuously improve their work, but also the 'permission' to make this their way of working. It is about shifting from a mind-set of "that's just the way things are", to one of "this is the way things could be"!

The approach and format for this workbook is much like that of my previous two. It can act as a refresher for people who have attended one of my workshops relating to operational excellence. It can be used as a stand-alone manual for individuals who wish to learn about how to continuously improve their work. It can also provide the basis for planning and facilitating workshops with others.

Please note that this book is an introduction to the discipline, and you might want to read around the subject, take some formal training, or use an accredited practitioner to support and mentor you on your further journey. Do get in touch if you would like us to help you with that.

Each chapter is designed to reflect my approach for running workshops in operational excellence. The first chapter provides the context and framework for starting any operational excellence initiative. The subsequent chapters are best followed sequentially as they will take you through the framework in a step-by-step way.

There are practical scenarios to show how the various principles and methodologies can be applied in almost any area of work where there is some form of repeated process. Each chapter has an exercise for practising the principles and methodologies, either in teams or individually. If you are using this book in teams, do allow plenty of time for the exercises and for discussion and reflection.

The workbook also includes support materials in the form of full-page versions of illustrations and tables for use as a team and for your individual planning.

Finally, there are references for further reading if you would like to find out more about the subject.

Introduction to the Practical Scenarios

I will be using the following practical scenarios throughout the book to show how the various principles and methodologies can be applied. These are the same three that I used in my previous book "The Effective Team's High Performance Workbook". They are partly based on real situations that I have encountered, but also adapted to better illustrate the points that I am making.

Scenario 1 – Defining a centralised (shared) business service

A new central library team has been pulled together from members of a number of previously decentralised service teams. The centralised team is responsible for core processes such as purchase of print and electronic resources, subscriptions and loans, and can learn from the good practices and also the issues encountered from the previous decentralised teams.

Scenario 2 – Enhancing the effectiveness of laboratory processes

A Life Science team is performing fairly well but the manager believes that the team could be raised to a higher level of performance. Applying Lean and Six Sigma techniques to discreet processes, such as those used in the labs, will be a way to reinforce other measures being adopted by the team to enhance its performance.

Scenario 3 - Refocusing the approach of an SME (Small or Medium Enterprise)

This organisation needs to substantially change its way of working. It has grown organically from an academic base, and needs to take a more business-like approach to enable some dramatic growth. The CEO believes that introducing "operational excellence" as a way of working will help to achieve that.

Chapter 1. The Context for your Journey

"Finding those hidden treasures"

Background and principles

Lean and Six Sigma

The principles, tools and techniques used in this book are derived from Lean and Six Sigma: approaches originally developed by Toyota and Motorola for application in the manufacturing industry, but translatable to any sector of work or indeed to everyday life. I often find myself in a hotel, restaurant, shop, office, or indeed in my own home or garden when I spot opportunities for improving the quality of customer service, the layout of the working area, or the approach to a process or task.

The focus of Lean is on the reduction of waste in time, cost and resources and on the optimum use of people's talents and creativity. Elimination of waste enables us to reduce the cost and time spent on processes. It relies on those involved in the process participating in its evaluation and in the identification of opportunities for simplifying and streamlining it. Lean also focuses on creating a smooth flow in operations and delivering a product or service based on the "pull" by the customer.

Six Sigma is about improving the quality of a product or service supplied to a customer by identifying and removing defects or errors, and reducing variation in that quality. It is based on the principle that what is defined as value is in the eye of the customer. It also makes use of statistical analysis, which is not something that is usually included in my workshops. I have included a brief summary of the meaning of 'Six Sigma' in the Appendix. See Munro et al in the Further Reading section if you who would like to find out more about it.

In this book I will be choosing and combining elements from both Lean and Six Sigma, with a minimal use of some of the associated terms and jargon. Readers looking for a more purist exposition may like to read Womack and Jones' book listed in the Further Reading section.

The mind set and principles for continuous improvement

Operational excellence relies on having an open and inquisitive mind. It is about recognising that everything we do is potentially very complex. It is a web of interaction between the people involved in the work, the processes that are being carried out and the environment that this all happens within. This complexity requires constant study, learning and improvement. In fact we could regard every problem that we find as a "treasure" that will help us to reduce the future need for fire fighting and associated stress. Those treasures might also include good practices that individuals have been adopting to address known issues, but that the rest of the team might not be aware of.

Every problem that we find and solve, and every good practice that we adopt will enable us to improve the quality of what we do, and reduce the demands on cost and time. Each "treasure" has the potential to improve our productivity, and to help us feel happier in our work!

Operational excellence is also a continuous journey: no sooner have we solved one problem, and implemented an associated solution than we are likely to find another. The essential is not be disheartened, but to recognise that this is part of the journey towards operational excellence.

This journey is also one that we cannot do alone. Each piece of work that we are engaged in is part of a bigger picture. It is part of an end-to-end process from the customers who define their expectations of a service or product, through to the team members involved in the associated process, and the suppliers who provide the necessary materials or information to make it happen. All those involved in a piece of work will have something to say about how it could be improved, and their buy-in is also essential to enable those improvements to be put in place.

Principle	In other words
Customers define the 'quality' of products and services.	Find out what is critical to your customers and embed this in the process.
The quality and speed of our work are optimised by: • Minimising variation • Eliminating wasted time, cost and effort.	Focus on these elements for improvement.
The flow and speed of our work is determined by customer 'pull'.	We should base our key performance indicators on what our customers have asked for, not what we think they might want.
Those doing the work have the best knowledge to improve the way it is done.	Involve those doing the work in finding and resolving problems. They are more likely to take ownership for implementing the solutions.
"Operational Excellence" is a continuous journey.	It is a mind-set, and a progressive approach over a long period of time will deliver the best results.

Table 1.1 Principles for operational excellence

DMAIC – a framework for continuous improvement

Operational excellence can be a 'point in time' business change project, but it is best undertaken as an on-going long-term approach. DMAIC (Define, Measure, Analyse, Improve, Control) provides a framework for managing it in both contexts, as shown in Figure 1.1.

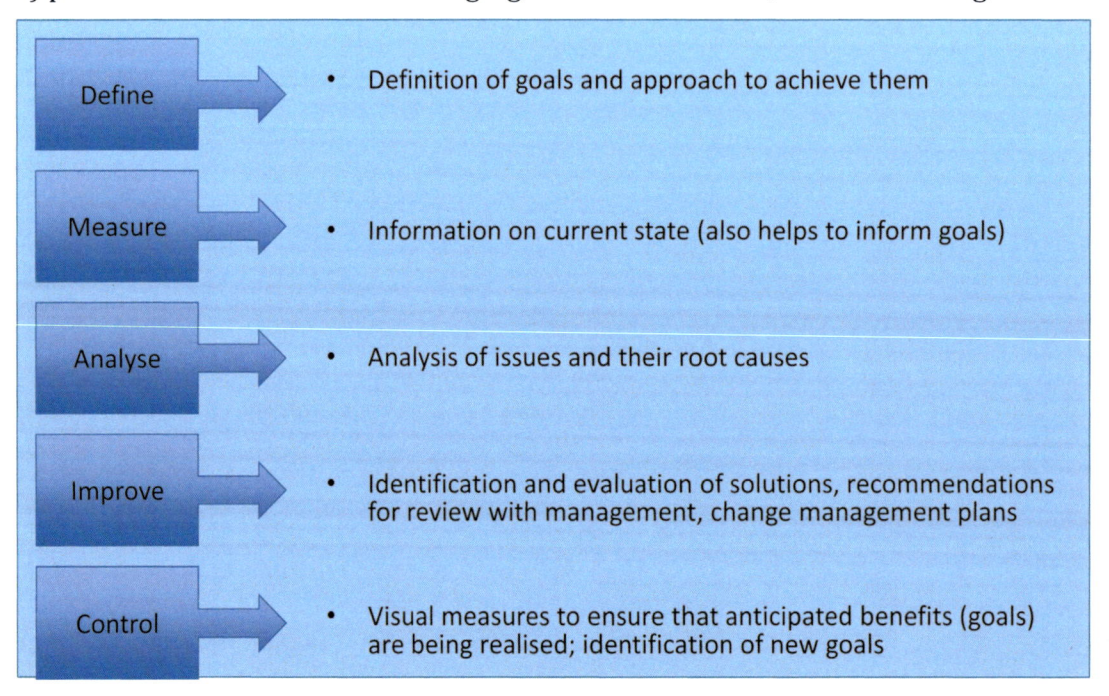

- Define → Definition of goals and approach to achieve them
- Measure → Information on current state (also helps to inform goals)
- Analyse → Analysis of issues and their root causes
- Improve → Identification and evaluation of solutions, recommendations for review with management, change management plans
- Control → Visual measures to ensure that anticipated benefits (goals) are being realised; identification of new goals

Figure 1.1 The DMAIC framework for managing operational excellence

Those of you familiar with project management will spot some parallels with and some differences from a typical project life cycle. The DMAIC framework emphasises the need for clear goals (or anticipated benefits) in the initial 'Define' phase. It uses facts and data – Measure - to understand the current state, identify potential solutions – Improve, and evaluate to what extent the anticipated benefits have been realised - Control. It also includes an 'Analyse' phase to identify the root causes for any issues. Involvement of all those concerned (the stakeholders) is paramount for managing the changes associated with implementation of the solutions.

The DMAIC framework can be applied at any level of granularity: in an overall operational excellence programme, or in individual improvement projects within the programme.

We will be considering each individual phase of the DMAIC in the next five chapters, but you may find it helpful to consider the context for your operational excellence journey in terms of the framework as a whole. Here is how it could be applied to the three scenarios.

Illustrations from the scenarios

Scenario 1 - Defining a centralised (shared) business service

Define: The goal for this scenario is to define the new centralised business service in a way that builds on the good practices of the previously decentralised processes. There is an overall driver of reducing costs, and of taking advantage of new technological advances. There are four core processes to be considered: the purchase of printed resources and of electronic resources, subscriptions and loans.

Measure: The teams already have data on customer requirements and on the performance of the previous ('as is') processes. They should check these data to ensure that there is enough there to inform the definition of the four future 'to be' processes.

Analyse: All the people involved in the previous processes, and in the new ones, will be able to explore the root causes of what has, and has not, worked well in the past.

Improve: The teams, their managers, suppliers and customers will all need to be engaged in defining and/or reviewing the way forward for the centralised service. The evaluation will include assessing the suitability and use of new externally available technological solutions.

Control: When defining the new centralised processes, the teams should identify some measures that will enable them to monitor how well they are meeting customer requirements (their effectiveness), and how efficient the processes are in terms of time, cost and resources. These measures will also enable the teams to continue to identify opportunities for improvement.

Scenario 2 – Enhancing the effectiveness of laboratory processes

Define: The Life Science team has chosen to focus on the effectiveness of its laboratory processes – are they delivering to customer requirements? Is the team being as productive as it could be?

Measure: There are data to be collected on customer requirements, and on the performance of the individual processes. The team may also like to consider whether the layout of its lab is as effective as it could be.

Analyse: All of the people engaged in the laboratory processes should be involved in exploring the root causes of any issues that may be preventing them from being as effective as they could be.

Improve: The team, its manager, suppliers and customers will all need to be engaged in defining and/or reviewing the way forward for the team's work.

Control: When defining any new approaches, the team members should identify some measures that will enable them to monitor how well they are meeting customer requirements (their effectiveness), and how efficient the processes are in terms of time, cost and resources. These measures will also enable the team to continue to identify opportunities for improvement.

Scenario 3 – Refocusing the approach of an SME (Small or Medium Enterprise)

Define: This organisation needs to make a significant shift in its way of working to drive business growth. This is a question of clearly defining its offering: what is required to deliver value to existing and prospective customers; as well as how it should be spending its time and money to deliver that value compared to what it is currently doing.

Measure: There are data to be collected on customer requirements, and on all aspects of how all members of the organisation are spending their time and resources.

Analyse: All of the people engaged in the work of the organisation should be involved in analysing the outcomes from the Measure phase.

Improve: The members of the organisation, the managers, suppliers and customers will all need to be engaged in defining and/or reviewing the way forward for the organisation.

Control: When defining any new approaches, individual teams should identify some measures that will enable them to monitor how well they are meeting customer requirements (their effectiveness), and how efficient the processes are in terms of time, cost and resources. These measures will also enable the organisation to continue to identify opportunities for improvement.

Individual or team exercise 1.1 What is the context for operational excellence in your organisation?

I am assuming that you are reading this book because you want to improve the effectiveness and efficiency of your own work, that of your team or your organisation's. A good place to start, before you even begin to address this, is to consider the context for your programme or project in terms of each step of the DMAIC. Reflect and jot down some notes as follows:

Define

What is the goal for your application of operational excellence? What benefits do you expect as a result?

Measure

What existing information or data do you have for what your customers expect from the products or services that are covered by your goal? What data do you have on the performance of the associated processes? Where might the gaps be? Who can provide the existing and missing data?

Analyse

Who are the people with the insights on the data for what is going well and what might need improving?

Improve

Who should be involved to shape and agree the new processes and solutions?

Control

What might be some ways to assess whether anticipated benefits are being realised, and to actively monitor new ways of working for further improvements?

Who will be the sponsor or sponsors for this work? Do you have the budget and the authority to involve the people above, or will you need the approval of your own and/or their line managers?

Use the notes you have made as the basis for exploratory conversations with the necessary sponsors and other individuals and for getting them engaged.

You might also want to refer to my earlier book "The Effective Team's Change Management Workbook" to help you with this and later steps for managing change.

Closing thoughts

It is possible to apply operational excellence at different levels of granularity: across the organisation as a whole, or for individual processes. As none of our work exists in isolation, the most effective approach will be an end-to-end one that addresses all the interdependencies within an organisation. However it may be more practical, as you start on your journey, to introduce operational excellence at a more tactical level within a specific department or team.

You may then be able to use your early results to demonstrate the value of operational excellence and get others excited about getting involved.

How long a full DMAIC cycle will take depends on the scale of the programme or project, and also on how long it takes to complete a cycle of any process being considered. The following is a very rough guideline on timings for a team project. Actual timings will depend on the complexity of the project and the availability of the people involved.

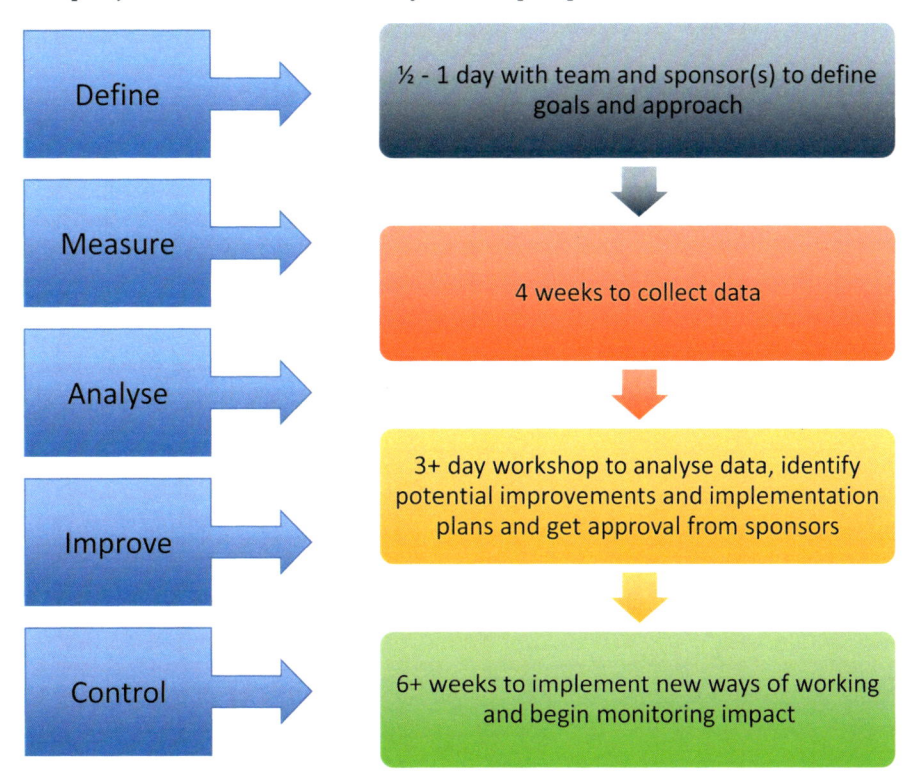

Figure 1.2 Rough timeline for an operational excellence project

Chapter 2. Working with your Customers

"Quality is in the eye of the beholder"

Background and principles

Defining your customers and understanding their expectations

Without our customers, we would not be in business. At the end of the day, they define why we do what we do, and the criteria for what we deliver. However, all too often, we approach things the other way around: we produce what we think is important, and we define our own criteria for a quality product or service. This chapter is about doing things differently and focusing our work on what constitutes value for our customers: the value stream.

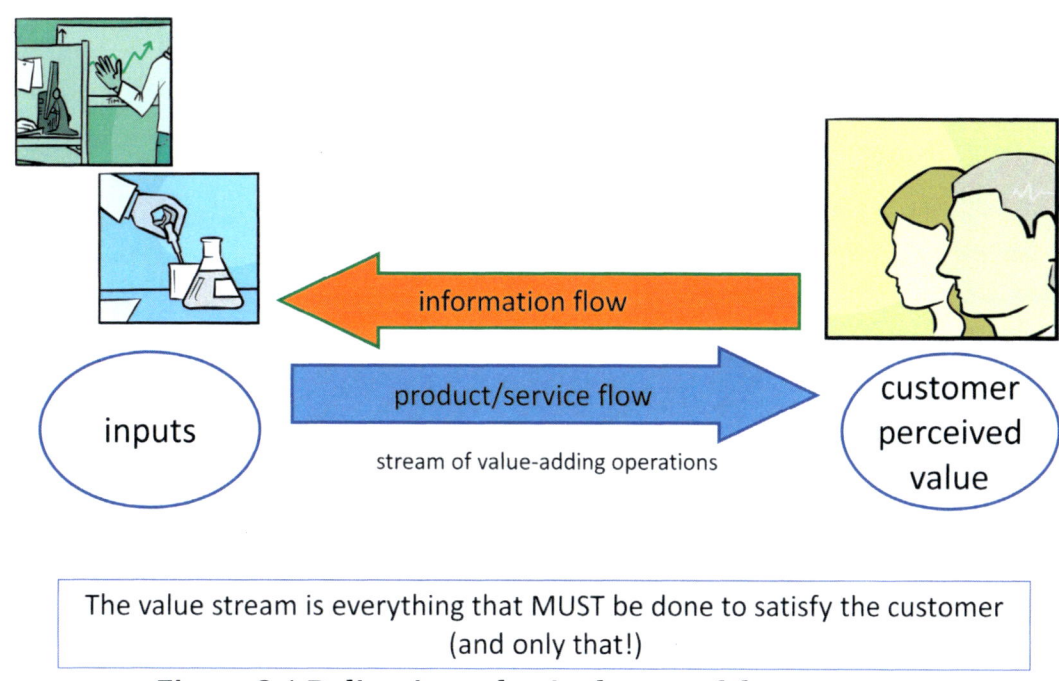

The value stream is everything that MUST be done to satisfy the customer (and only that!)

Figure 2.1 Delivering value in the eye of the customer

We all have multiple customers for our products or services, so that it can be difficult to determine which customers to focus on to prioritise and meet their requirements. It can help to think of our customers in terms of 'big C' and 'little c' customers. 'Big C' customers are the ultimate users of our organisation's products or services. They choose, pay for and use what our organisation produces. 'Little c' customers are those that help to deliver the product or service. They help deliver ultimate value to the 'big C' customers. Customers can be internal as well as external. Internal customers will be colleagues within our own or other departments.

Examples of 'big C' and 'little c' customers, and of internal and external customers are shown in tables 2.1 – 2.3.

We might assume that we know what our customers' requirements are. However there are many ways to determine their true requirements and to hear "the voice of the customer". Whilst a popular method is to use surveys, we are lucky if we get a 30% response rate when using them. The most effective method is one-to-one dialogue. It will take more of our time, but our customers will appreciate the attention and the quality of the information obtained and the resultant enhancement of customer relationships will make it worthwhile. Of course the more customers we have, the more we will have to resort to just selecting a sample to speak to, and perhaps use a survey to reach a larger number, or to get more of a cross-section of views on some specific questions. Figure 2.2 summarises the different ways to collect input and feedback from customers.

I worked with one CRO (Contract Research Organisation) who decided to survey its globally dispersed customers by giving them the option of telephone interviews, or online questionnaires. This was during an Easter break and at the time of the Icelandic volcano eruption when the ash in the atmosphere severally affected airline flights. Many of the CRO's contacts were stranded in their holiday destinations but they asked if the interviews could be scheduled for their return. As a result, the CRO obtained a 60% response rate to their survey. In addition, they not only found out what their customers valued, but introduced the customers to services that they had not previously been aware of. They also generally boosted the quality of their relationships. Carrying out this survey produced a real high of satisfaction amongst the CRO staff involved.

There are many ways to hear the "Voice of the Customer"

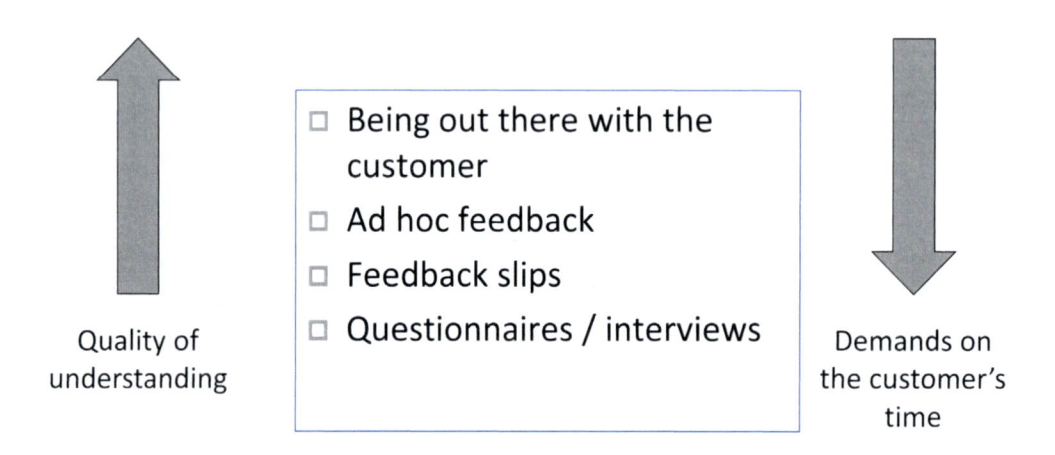

- Being out there with the customer
- Ad hoc feedback
- Feedback slips
- Questionnaires / interviews

Quality of understanding ↑

Demands on the customer's time ↓

Are you doing this effectively for your key products or services?

Figure 2.2 Alternative approaches for determining customer requirements

'SIPOC' - a framework for improving processes and projects

The term SIPOC is an acronym for Supplier, Inputs, Process, Outputs, Customer (or stakeholder). It is a useful tool at the start of any initiative to help define the context for what is being done. It can be used at whatever level of granularity is most helpful to the people involved. It can for example be used to describe a business, the on-going work of an operational team, a project, or even a specific meeting.

Used well, a SIPOC helps a team or an organisation to consider why and how they are doing something from a customer's point of view, rather than from the more common and limited focus of the process (or processes) they are working on. Just completing a SIPOC should enable a team to discover opportunities for improvement in the quality of and approach to what they are doing. A template for producing a SIPOC is shown in Figure 2.3

Suppliers	Inputs	Process	Outputs	Customers
Who are our suppliers?	What do we need to carry out our process effectively and efficiently?	What are the key steps involved to produce what the customers want? (The value stream)	What do our clients want in terms of products, services and quality?	Who are our customers?

FINISH ←———————————————————————— START

Figure 2.3 The SIPOC framework for improving an area of work

Customers. We have already discussed the different types of customers. Whether your customers are 'big C' or 'little c', you will find it most helpful, when completing a SIPOC to consider the most immediate customers for your products, services, or project.

Outputs are the customers' requirements. They may include data or information as well as more tangible outputs. Customers' expectations of quality will include specific timelines, budgetary constraints, and other criteria for quality typically associated with your product or service.

Here are some examples of criteria for products that you might use in discussions with your customers (see Munro et al):

- Performance
- Benefit relative to cost
- Durability
- Safety
- Serviceability
- Usability / ease of use
- Simplicity of design
- Functionality
- Availability

And here are some (from the same source) that you might use for services:

- Responsiveness
- Reliability
- Competence
- Access
- Communication
- Credibility / image
- Confidentiality / security
- Understanding the customer
- Accuracy / completeness
- Timeliness

Process. The definition of the process, for now, includes the key five to seven steps that will deliver the customer's requirements. These key steps are also known as the value stream. They are the essential steps that will transform the customers' requirements and raw materials for the product or service, into the tangible deliverable that the customer requested.

Ideally there will be a final sign off step from the customer to confirm that what they requested has been delivered. This could be a signature on receipt, or some more formal feedback.

Inputs are the raw materials for the value stream. Again they may include information, and will have attached criteria for the timeliness, cost and quality that you expect from your suppliers.

Suppliers are the final component of the SIPOC. These may be internal colleagues as well as external suppliers. Your customers are also suppliers as you are relying on them to provide information and criteria for your value stream.

Illustrations from the scenarios

As you will see from Tables 2.1, 2.2 and 2.3, you will need to make choices about what aspects of your operational excellence programme, your customers, outputs and processes to focus on at each stage of the SIPOC. You may choose to complete a series of SIPOCs to address each of these different aspects of your work.

Suppliers	Inputs	Process	Outputs (examples)	Customers
Users of the service Publishers / suppliers of printed and electronic sources Team members IT department Managers and external professional colleagues	Customer requirements List of available sources Team members' expertise for search strategies Appropriate technology for managing daily alerts Constraints and opportunities relating to use of resources	Focusing on one of the outputs – the daily alerts: 1. Establish customer requirements 2. Identify relevant sources 3. Develop search strategy 4. Set up daily alert 5. Periodically review and revise approach to ensure sources and search strategy continue to meet customer requirements, and are making best use of the resources available	Focusing on the 'big C' customers only: Daily alerts to the latest competitor, legal and other information in their area of expertise that may have significant impact on their work. Direct access to the core publications for their disciplines within a week of their publication. The ability to retrieve bibliographic citations and full text sources for key references when undergoing new areas of research	All members of the organisation who use the services ('big C'). Colleagues in the decentralised teams ('little c') acting as intermediaries for the other customers.

**Table 2.1 SIPOC for Scenario 1 –
Defining a centralised (shared) business service**

Suppliers	Inputs	Process	Outputs (examples)	Customers
Internal colleagues Internal and external (published) information resources Team members Laboratory suppliers Managers and external professional colleagues	Customer requirements Previously developed SOPs Information on potential alternative procedures Team members' expertise for carrying out these tests Appropriate laboratory facilities and reagents Constraints and opportunities relating to use of resources	1. Establish customer requirements 2. Identify appropriate SOP (Standard Operating Procedure) or alternative procedure(s) to carry out the required test(s). 3. Ensure all necessary reagents and test conditions are available and schedule the test(s) 4. Carry out the test(s) 5. Deliver test results with appropriate background information 6. Periodically review and revise approach to ensure tests used and associated information continue to meet customer requirements, and are making best use of the resources available	Focusing on the 'little c' customers only: Rapid turn-around of test results. Proactive suggestions of alternative tests and other background information that might be worth considering.	External clients for whom the team is carrying out these processes ('big C'). Colleagues in other departments ('little c') who rely on the team's data in order to complete their work for external clients.

Table 2.2 SIPOC for Scenario 2 - Enhancing the effectiveness of laboratory processes

Suppliers	Inputs	Process	Outputs (examples)	Customers
Existing and potential clients Staff / managers Internal and external information resources Managers and staff (plus consultants?) Laboratory and office suppliers	Customer requirements Data on current performance Competitive intelligence Internal and 'little c' expertise Available people and facilities to implement required changes	1. Establish customer requirements 2. Evaluate how the organisation is currently delivering against those requirements 3. Benchmark against other similar organisations 4. Define what / how the organisation could work differently to become 'best in class' relative to customer requirements 5. Develop implementation plans in consultation with 'little c' customers 6. Implement, monitor / review	Competitive timelines, quality and / or cost of service relative to alternative suppliers	Existing and potential external clients of the SME's products and services ('big C'). Board and/or executive management team ('little c').

Table 2.3 SIPOC for Scenario 3 – Refocusing the approach of an SME (Small or Medium Enterprise)

Team exercise 2.1 Construct a SIPOC

Step 1.

Assemble the team of people who are going to be involved in your operational excellence programme or project. Use this workbook, and your reflections from Team exercise 1.1 to give them some background on your operational excellence project.

Step 2.

Prepare a SIPOC on a flipchart (or use a copy of the full-page version at the end of this book) based on the focus for operational excellence that you selected in Chapter 1.

- Consider who is / are the customers of your product, service or project
- What are their desired outputs and what criteria have the customers specified in terms of time, cost or quality?
- Describe the key steps in your process for delivering these outputs (5-7 high level steps)
- What are the inputs and what are your criteria for these?
- Who supplies the input?

You may not immediately know the answers to all of these questions. How could you find out?

Step 3.

Gaining greater insights from your customers. Would one-to-one conversations with your customers or use of a representative sample be helpful here? Should you support this with a survey? (See the closing thoughts below for one approach to a survey.)

Step 4.

Final reflections: what else have you discovered from carrying out this exercise?

Closing thoughts

It is important to choose the right focus for improvement.

For Scenario 1 this is very clear: it is the four processes that are to be centralised.

The scope of Scenario 2 is broader as it could cover a large number of processes being carried out in the lab, as well as the physical layout of the lab.

Scenario 3 has the broadest scope of all, so that another technique: 'Activity and Customer Value Analysis' (or ACVA) could be helpful here as shown in Figure 2.4. As the name implies, the ACVA combines an analysis of the activities that the team is carrying out (and the resources spent on each), with an assessment of their relative value by the customer. This analysis enables the team to make an informed decision about how to prioritise its time or resources going forward.

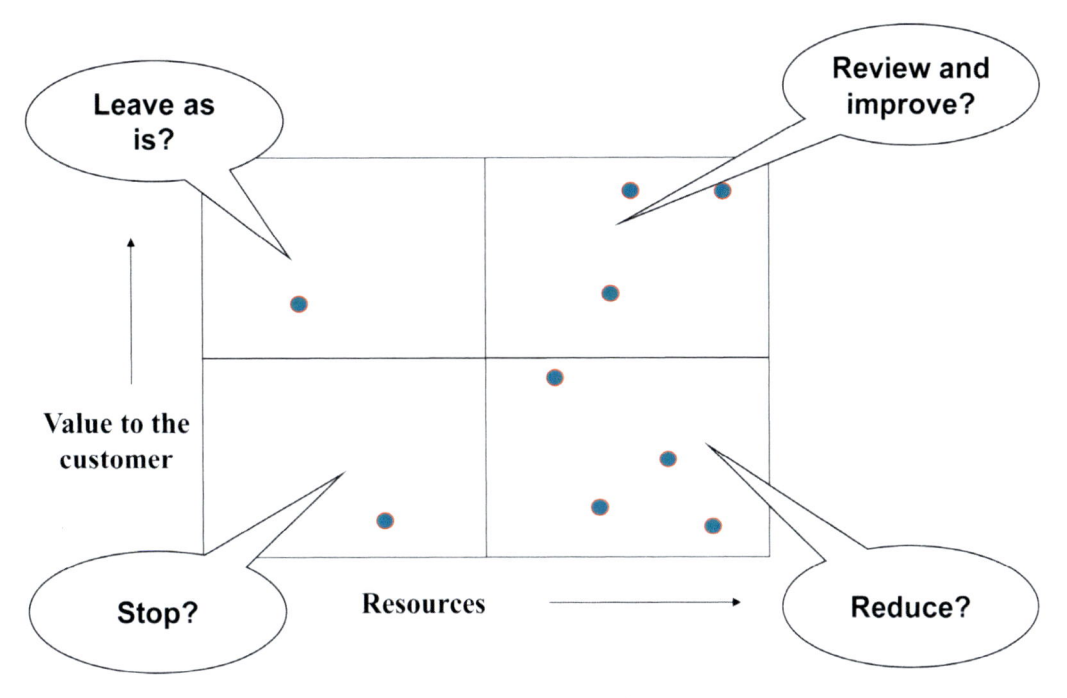

Figure 2.4 An ACVA diagram

The ACVA technique is not something that I routinely cover in my workshops, but I have included it here as you may find carrying out at a version of this very helpful. I have also included my case study with an Information Analysis department in the Further Reading section.

Reviewing the team's priorities in an ACVA study

Would you like to conduct a study on how the team as a whole is spending its time as in Scenario 3? In which case you will need the timesheet described in the next chapter, in Table 3.2. A full-page version is available in the Appendix but you might like to use an electronic copy (for example in Excel) as this will be easier to use with a large volume of data. I will work through the steps shown in Figure 2.5.

Collecting activity data

```
1. Identify processes and activities
    2. Decide approach for data collection
        3. Pilot the approach
            4. Collect the data
                5. Check for completeness
                    6. Collate and analyse
```

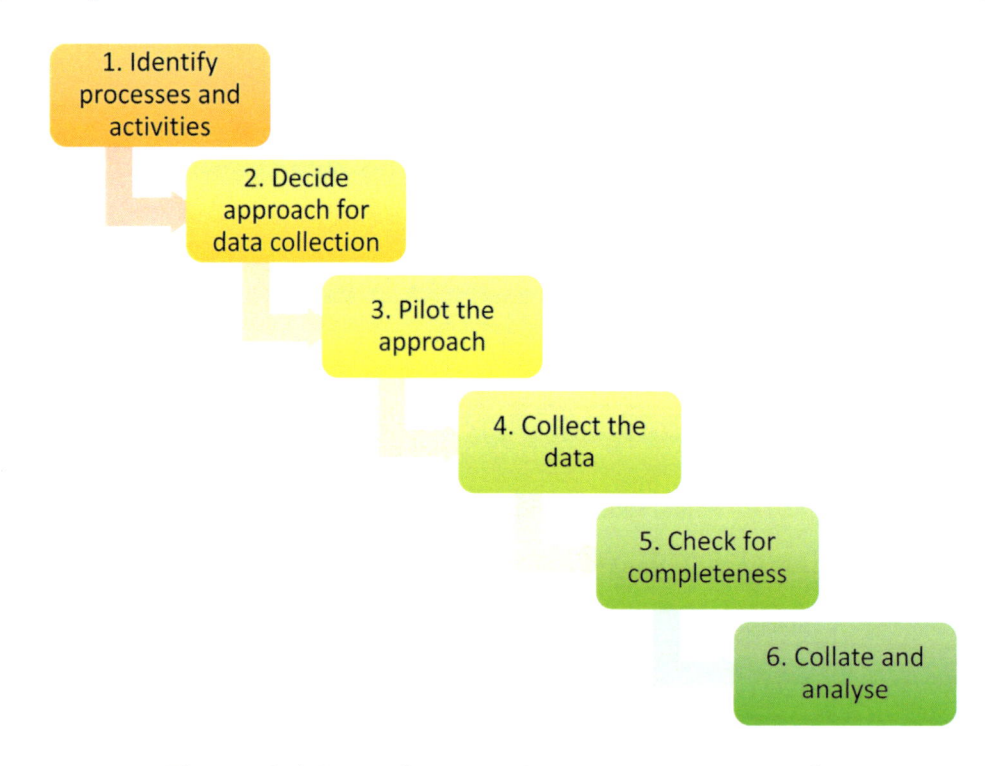

Figure 2.5 Steps for carrying out an ACVA study

Step 1. Identify processes and activities. Identify all of the processes that you carry out, whether documented in SOPs (Standard Operating Procedures) or not. These can be internal or management processes such as completing monthly reports, carrying out staff appraisals, learning and development, as well as those involved in producing your products and services.

Give each process a standard name.

Identify as many activities within these processes as you can think of. Examples of activities for staff appraisals would be: collecting customer input, preparing written input for the appraisal, conducting the appraisal, writing up the outputs. Give these activities standard names too.

Collate a list of all the processes and activities in your spreadsheet, with drop down menus, if working electronically, to facilitate their use.

Include 'other' categories to allow for new processes and activities that you might have missed.

Step 2. Decide on the approach for data collection. Decide how you are going to collect the data, for how many days, and whether to do so continuously or on a sampling basis.

Will you observe each other or have each person collect the data individually? Remember that the data are likely to be more complete if you use an observer, but you may not have the time and resources to do this.

Step 3. Pilot the approach. Pilot the data collection before continuing in earnest. This will help you to test and address the questions about your approach as suggested in Step 2.

It will also help you to pick up other processes and activities that you have missed, although you should still retain the 'other' category.

Step 4. Collect the data. Collect the data and have someone centrally monitor how this is going so as to be able to adjust approaches as needed.

Step 5. Check for completeness. Are there any processes or activities that may be under-represented for instance because they are once yearly or quarterly events, or only happen very occasionally? Add these to your data pool.

Step 6. Collate and analyse. Collate the results of all of your observations. You might like to represent them as histograms to show a) the amount of time spent on each process; b) the amount of time spent on each activity within each process.

Use the ACVA 4-box plot to help you decide how you will manage your resources based on the outcome of the study

Put together a plan for taking this forward

Collecting customer value data.

The consultation with the customer could take the form of a structured interview or questionnaire with the following content:

1. *A list of all your known activities* – with brief descriptions to inform or remind your customers about them.
2. *Some form of prioritisation by the customer*: they could rate the relative importance of each activity on a scale of say one to ten; or you could ask them to tell you which should be stopped or continued, and which new activities they would like you to start.
3. *Suggestions for what could be improved and how.*
4. *Confirmation of anything that you are currently doing particularly well, and in what way.*

Analysing the results.

Compare your customers' responses with the data on your activities, using the ACVA 4-box plot as shown in Figure 2.4. This will enable you to make informed decisions about:
- Activities that are valued by the customer that you could usefully focus on more
- Activities that are valued by the customer that might be worth streamlining or improving in some way
- Activities that are not valued by the customer and that you should perhaps stop altogether
- Activities that are not valued by the customer, but have some other operational value and so could also be streamlined to reflect their lower priority

The results of this analysis could become the focus for individual operational excellence programmes or projects that you could define and then take through the rest of the DMAIC process.

Chapter 3. Gathering Data

"Perception is not reality"

Background and principles

Operational excellence relies on having clear targets for performance, and tangible data to identify where performance falls short of those targets and to what extent.

You may not know what those targets for performance should be: setting them will be a combination of understanding your customer requirements, as we discussed in Chapter 2, and knowing what your processes are capable of, which is what you will need to measure.

Performance is typically measured in terms of time, cost or quality. These measures may relate to the final output of your product or service, as we discussed when doing the SIPOCs in Chapter 1, and are also referred to as output or outcome measures.

Performance may also be measured in terms of in-process metrics: what is happening in the intermediate steps leading to your output. The advantage of these in-process, or lead metrics is that they enable you to adjust what you are doing as you are doing it, and so have more certainty of achieving your final performance goals.

The Gemba or timesheet

There are a number of tools available to enable you to measure your performance. The first that our workshop delegates find most useful is the Gemba – the only Japanese term that I will refer to in this workbook! It means "the real place", or going to the actual place where the job is being done to observe the work.

There are typically at least three versions of what is happening with the process as shown in Figure 3.1. The first version is the one that is typically recorded in an SOP (Standard Operating Procedure) and that people would like to be happening. The second version is the one that people might believe is happening, as SOPs are not always followed to the letter. The third version is likely to be the actual truth, including issues that arise and work-arounds and improvements that people have introduced over time.

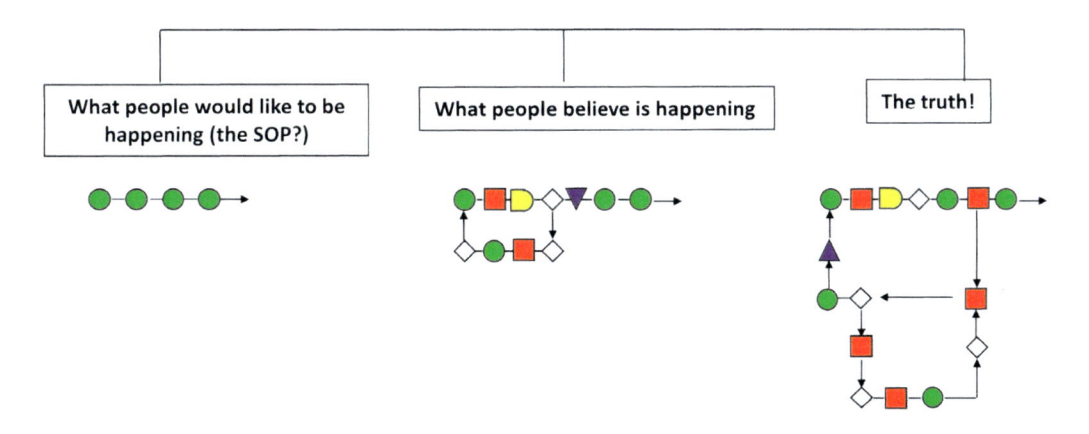

Figure 3.1 The various representations of a process

We use a timesheet, as shown in Table 3.1, to collect facts and data, rather than rely on perception, and so understand what is actually happening as a process is being carried out. The format that is typically used to collect the data is a paper-based or electronic spreadsheet. Table 3.1 has examples filled in for Scenario 1.

Step	Description	Start time	End time	Total time (minutes)	Delay (minutes)
1	Establish customer requirements	11:00	11:30	30	0
2	Identify relevant sources	12:30	12:45	15	60
3	Check that the right sources have been selected	13:30	13:50	20	45
4	Develop search strategy	13:50	14:20	30	0
5	Review results & strategy with customer	14:40	15:10	30	20
6	Set up daily alert	15:30	15:50	20	20

Table 3.1 A timesheet for collecting data on a process – with examples from Scenario 1

Ideally, you would collect at least three iterations of a particular process using this timesheet. Every single step would be recorded, including any that are not in the formal SOP. It is these variations in the process that are going to be of most interest for our analysis.

The units of time in Table 3.1 are in minutes, but they could be in hours, days, weeks or months depending on the process. Any individual step could also span more than one day.

The delay column is also a useful source of data for the Analyse phase as I will describe in the next chapter.

The action of collecting data in this way will start raising team members' awareness of issues in the process that they may have previously been only partially aware of. It is important to record these issues too as part of the preparation for the analysis phase.

It is also important at this stage to remember the mind-set for operational excellence. This is about collecting those hidden treasures that will enable the team as a whole to improve the way it works. It is not a witch-hunt or an occasion to allocate blame. So it is a manager's role to help individuals feel safe about collecting the data. One way to do this is through role modeling by the team leader, or by making the data anonymous – though this is often not possible.

We did all of these things for the ACVA case study mentioned in the Closing thoughts of the previous chapter. We used a modified version of the timesheet to collect data on how the team as a whole was spending its time.

In the case study, the team identified some generic processes that described all of its work, and then recorded the time spent on individual activities associated with each of the generic processes. I acted as an external observer for how the Head of the Department spent every moment of his time, and we then shared that with the rest of the team to demonstrate the 'safety' of doing so.

Table 3.2 is a theoretical example of an ACVA style timesheet as it might look at the end of a senior manager's day.

Step	Process	Activity	Start time	End time	Total time (minutes)	Delay (minutes)
1	General Admin	Review / plan diary engagements for coming week	09:00	09:30	30	0
2	Staff Management	Prepare for performance reviews (3 staff)	09:30	10:30	60	0
3	Staff Management	Conversations with staff (in corridor)	10:30	10:45	15	0
4	Business Development	Meeting with potential new client	11:00	12:15	75	15
5	Staff Management	Conversations with staff (over lunch)	12:30	13:15	45	15
6	Professional Development	Read new issues of technical journals	13:15	13:45	30	0
7	Strategic Planning	Review budget forecasts against revenue	14:00	15:30	90	15
8	R&D	Discuss results vs. plans for project x	15:30	16:30	60	0
9	General Admin	Miscellaneous correspondence	16:45	17:15	30	15

Table 3.2 A timesheet for collecting data on all of an individual's or team's activities – with examples from Scenario 3

In the case study, team members were paired up to observe each other's work, and the results were collated so that the emphasis was not on individual behaviour, but on how the team as a whole was spending its time.

Spaghetti diagram

This is a relatively simple tool that can be used to measure the amount of movement that is taking place during a process. As the name implies, the resultant picture is often very much like a bundle of spaghetti that has been thrown up in the air and dropped. It can be used to represent virtual movement (i.e. electronic or information based) as well as physical movement. It leads to the possibility of organising the workplace or the flow of information more effectively, as shown in the before and after views in Figure 3.2. The 'after' scenario, where the work is streamlined from start to finish is known as 'cellular flow'.

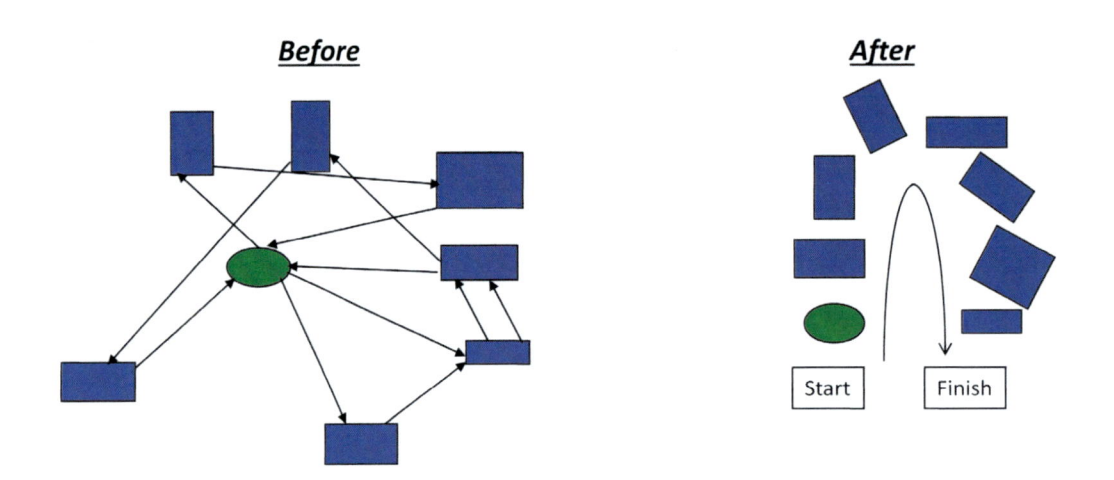

**Figure 3.2 A spaghetti diagram before and after reorganising
a workplace into cellular flow**

To create a spaghetti diagram for a physical workplace, produce a to scale drawing of the workplace, then follow the same procedure as for the timesheet, to document every single step in the process. Recording is done on the drawing itself (producing the 'before' result in Figure 3.2), making sure that every single movement is recorded and/or on a further adapted version of the timesheet with a column to record distance travelled for each step as shown in Table 3.3 with examples from Scenario 2.

Step	Activity	Distance (metres)	Start time	End time	Total time (minutes)	Delay (minutes)
1	Establish customer requirements (from e-mail notification)	0	09:00	09:15	15	0
2	Identify appropriate SOP or alternative procedure(s) to carry out the required test(s) (on office computer)	0	09:30	09:45	15	15
3	Ensure all necessary reagents are available (at freezer then lab bench)	5	09:45	10:00	15	0
4	Ensure all necessary test conditions are available (at fume cupboard)	2	10:00	10:15	15	0
5	Schedule the test (back at office computer)	3	10:15	10:35	20	0
6	Carry out the test (freezer, lab bench, fume cupboard)	7	14:05	15:20	75	210
7	Write up results (back at office computer)	5	15:40	16:40	60	20
8	Deliver test results with appropriate background information (by e-mail)	0	16:40	17:00	20	0

Table 3.3 A timesheet with column for physical motion data – with examples from Scenario 2

If the process in question is a virtual one, then the data to be collected is a list of all the individuals or departments involved and the movements between them in the information flow. Here it is not the distance travelled that is important, so much as the number of iterations between all the people concerned. This can also be captured in an adapted version of the timesheet as shown in Table 3.4 with examples from Scenario 1.

Step	Description	From / To	Start time	End time	Total time (minutes)	Delay (minutes)
1	Establish customer requirements	Customer to Analyst	11:00	11:30	30	0
2	Identify relevant sources	Analyst	12:30	12:45	15	60
3	Check that the right sources have been selected	Analyst to Manager	13:30	13:50	20	45
4	Develop search strategy	Analyst	13:50	14:20	30	0
5	Review results & strategy with customer	Analyst to Customer	14:40	15:10	30	20
6	Set up daily alert	Analyst	15:30	15:50	20	20

Table 3.4 A timesheet with column for virtual motion data – with examples from Scenario 1

The data collected will also be converted to a spaghetti diagram but this time it will be in the form of a 'swim lane' representation, where each individual or department occupies a 'lane' as in a swimming pool, as shown in Figure 3.3.

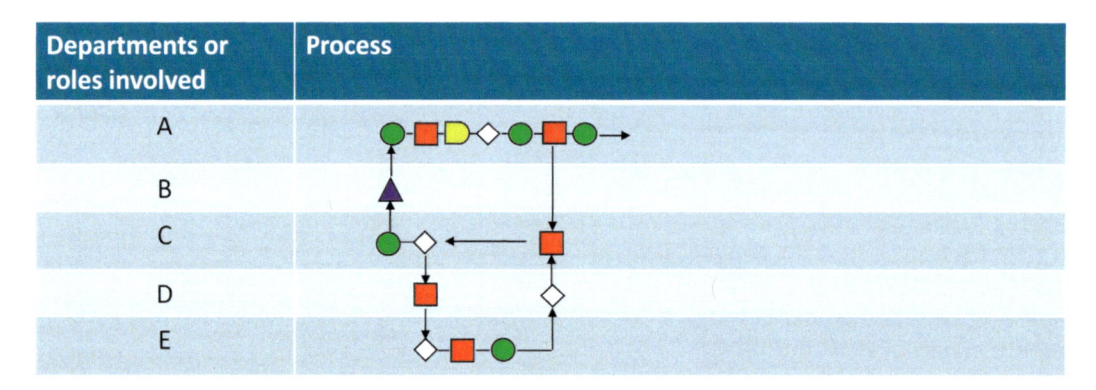

Figure 3.3 Swim lane representation of the flow of information or activities between individuals or departments in a process

This form of representation can obviously be used to show the different people involved in the various steps of a physical as well as a virtual process.

The drawing of the spaghetti diagram and swim lane representations can be left to the Analyse phase described in the next chapter. For now, the most important is to collect the data on what is actually happening in the process, and the timings and motion involved.

It is important to collect at least three iterations to gather as many instances of issues or good practices encountered as possible. In some cases, the process will vary depending on the nature of the client, or there may be different categories of requests. In this case it is important to collect examples of those different types of work too.

If the time that the process takes is longer than that available to carry out your operational excellence project, then you might have to look for historical data in your records to fill in some of the gaps. In fact, historical data may be a useful resource for processes of any duration.

Team exercise 3.1 Collect your data

Use your reflections from Chapter 2 to identify what you would like to focus on. If you would like to review how the team is spending its time as a whole, as in Scenario 3, then turn back to the Closing thoughts in Chapter 2 on conducting an ACVA. Otherwise, follow these steps to explore a specific process.

Step 1. Select the process to explore.

With your team, identify one important and/or frequently used process or procedure that you would like to explore with a view to identifying and implementing potential improvements to it. If you would like to explore more than one process, then agree to either do this sequentially or, if there are enough of you with the time and knowledge to split into small groups, agree to do these in parallel.

When you select the procedure or process make sure that:

- At least one member of the group knows the process inside out. The rest of the group is made up of a mixture of people who are directly involved in the process, and others who can bring a fresh perspective to it. It is important to brief everyone thoroughly on the process so that they are comfortable working on it for this exercise.
- The first process that you select should not be one that you have already spent a lot of time reviewing / improving. You will get more impact from your learning if you start with one that has had less attention.
- The first process should also be complex enough to give you something to 'get your teeth into' but also simple enough to enable everyone to 'get their heads around it' and get a tangible result.

Step 2. Collect the following information for that process or procedure:

a. An SOP (Standard Operating Procedure) or equivalent
b. A drawing of the layout of the working area (this is likely to be most relevant for a laboratory or other physically based process)
c. A list of all the people involved if the process is more 'virtual' than physical (this is more likely for an office or information based process)
d. An actual timeline (elapsed time) of all the steps involved for the process, with motion data too as appropriate. (You use a copy of the relevant full- page version of the timesheet in the Appendix, or work in Excel.)

The data you collect will form the basis of the Analyse phase of the DMAIC, as described in the next chapter.

Closing thoughts

'5S' is another tool that can be used for organising a physical workplace. It is a simple (some would say commonsensical) and low cost approach to creating an efficient and productive workplace. The principles can also be applied to an electronic workplace, but I will just focus on physical ones here.

Like many of the other tools in this book, it has Japanese origins, but we can use the terms in English as shown in Figure 3.4.

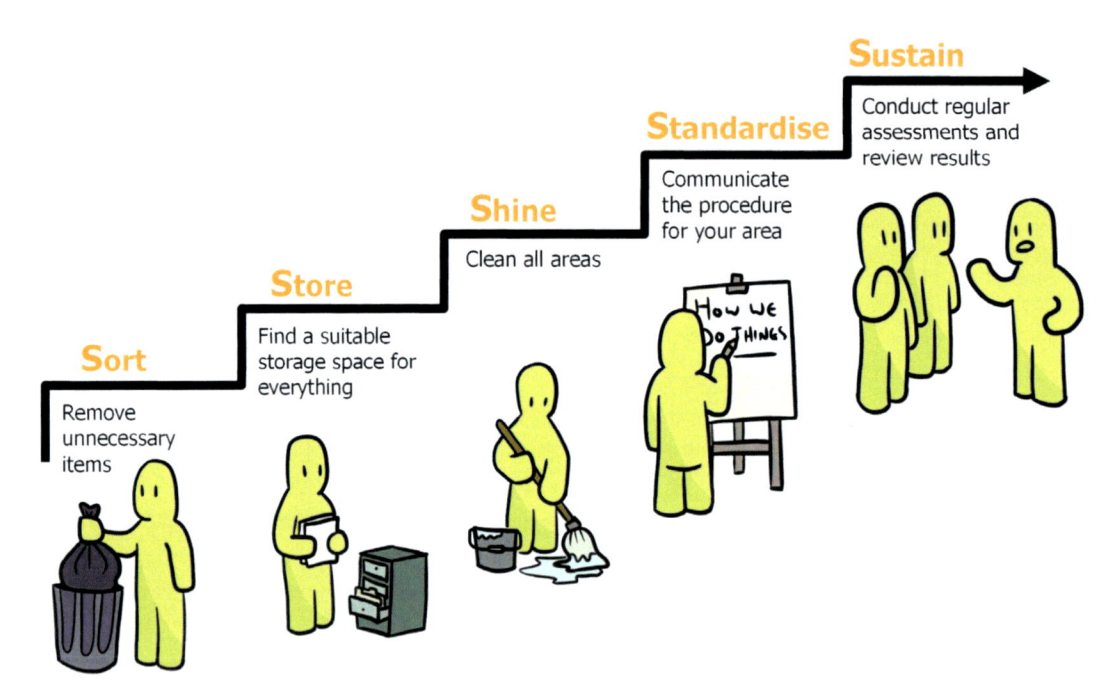

Figure 3.4 '5S'

Sort is about ensuring that all necessary equipment, materials and other resources, and only those, are held and available in the workplace. This means that time is not lost looking for things that should be there, and things that should not be there are not cluttering up the workplace.

A 'red tag' system is used: a red tag is attached to anything that is not essential to the work but still believed to be necessary, and these items are placed in a holding area. Red-tagged items are reviewed after a week, and a decision then made to dispose of them, or to relocate them to a storage area for more infrequent use.

The sort step is a useful one for clearing out any time sensitive or out-of-date items.

This step should be repeated at regular intervals, and at least every 6 months.

Holding areas should have designated managers who monitor movement in and out of the holding area, and ensure regular review and disposal or relocation of the contents.

Store is about organising the items that are retained in a way that will make them easy to find, use and put away.

Everything is neatly stored in a place that is aligned to the workflow, and within arm's reach.

Items are labeled with their physical location so that, if misplaced, they can be easily returned to the right place.

Storage areas can be demarcated with signs above or below them, with coloured coding or with tape on the floor.

Figure 3.5 shows some examples of storage areas before and after '5S' exercises.

Figure 3.5 Illustrations showing settings before and after '5S'

Shine is about making sure that the workplace is clean and free of litter, and that equipment is in good order. It is about everyone having a mindset of routine tidiness and cleanliness as well as possibly having designated responsibilities and schedules for this.

There is a link here with safety, as spillages and obstacles can cause accidents as well as potentially impact the quality of products and services.

Some environments may require signed record sheets to demonstrate that this step is being performed.

Standardise is about creating a set of agreed, documented and visible work practices that ensures that everyone is carrying out the previous three steps in a consistent way.

Sustain is about ensuring that '5S' continues to happen. Ways to do this include: involving everyone at the start to get their buy-in, communicating and celebrating progress and achievements, carrying out periodic audits to monitor what is happening, and all the other enabling approaches typically used when introducing new ways of working.

What opportunities might you have for implementing '5S' in your place of work?

What, if any, barriers might you encounter?

Chapter 4. Treating the Root Cause

"Dig deep enough and the solution will be obvious"

Background and principles

Having collected all of your data in the Measure phase of DMAIC, the next step is to analyse the data to discover the opportunities for improvement and how to address them.

You need first to represent all the data that you have collected in a meaningful way. We use a lot of visual tools for this.

Representing the process flow

Figure 3.1 showed the different ways that the same process could be represented. The data that you have collected should enable you to document what has actually been happening with your process. The best way to do this is to use 'Post-it' notes, and to write each individual step of the process on one 'Post-it'. You then affix all of the notes to a large sheet of paper, drawing connecting arrows to represent the direction of the process flow.

If you have collected data for more than one iteration of the process, and there are variations in the steps involved, then you can document those variations on individual 'Post-it' notes too, and site them beneath a main representation of the process as shown in Figure 4.1, using data from Scenario 2.

Figure 4.1 Using 'Post-it' notes to represent all of the actual steps in a process – illustrated with Scenario 2

You will see that I have annotated the 'Post-it' notes with the timings collected during the Measure phase, and also showed a couple of variations in the steps (on the orange 'Post-it' notes) from different iterations of the process. There would usually also be some variation in the actual timings for each step.

Using time-value maps

Our processes as we practise them include:

- Value adding steps
- Non-value adding steps
- Non-value adding but necessary steps
- Waiting

Sometimes it helps to use an analogy such as making a cup of tea to help explain the distinction between these.

Value-adding steps are all those that are needed to transform the inputs to the process into the desired outputs. For this we need to:

- Find out the customer's requirements (what type of tea would they like, of what strength, with / without milk and sugar, with a teapot or not, with a cup or mug etc.)
- Infuse the tea for the appropriate length of time in suitably hot water
- Put it in the required receptacle
- Add the required milk / sugar
- Deliver it to the customer ensuring that it meets their requirements

Value-adding steps are also described as those that the customer would be prepared to pay for to ensure they get what they want.

Non-value adding steps are, by definition, those involving time spent that the customer would not be prepared to pay for. These would include for instance:

- Going to the corner shop because you've run out of tea, milk or sugar
- Taking crockery or cutlery out of cupboards and drawers
- Waiting for the kettle to boil
- Washing up or putting rubbish out
- Waiting for access to the tea making work area
- Having to remake the tea because the tea bag has split
- Etc.

Some of these steps are **necessary** because you would not be able to make the tea without them, and some of them involve **waiting**.

A streamlined process eliminates or reduces the non-value adding steps. A time-value map helps you to visualise the opportunities for doing so, as shown in the abstract in Figure 4.2, and using Scenario 2 as an example in Figure 4.3.

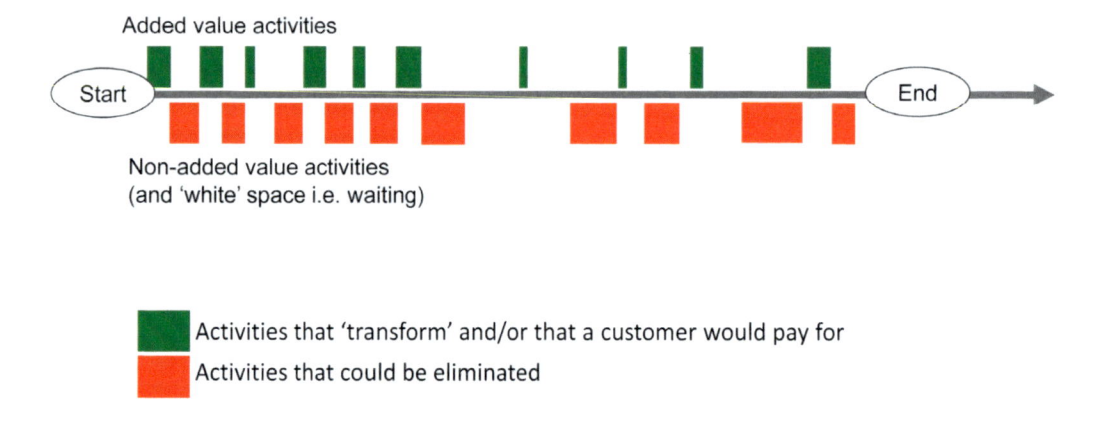

Figure 4.2 A time-value map

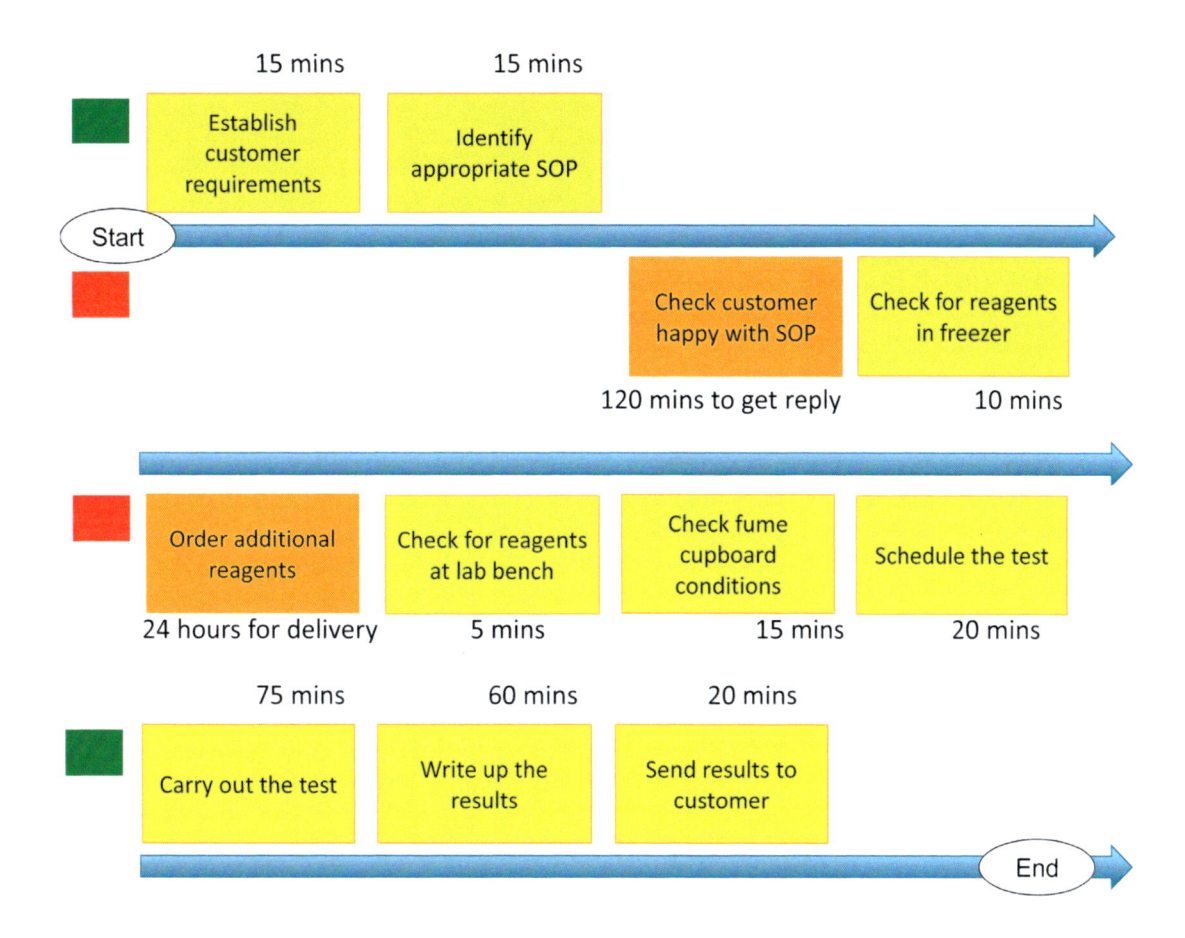

Figure 4.3 A time-value map for a process from Scenario 2

There is typically a lot of debate within a team as to which steps are value adding as opposed to non-value adding but necessary. It is not essential to get agreement. What is important is for the team to use this as an opportunity to thoroughly consider the opportunities for beginning to simplify and streamline their processes.

Spaghetti diagrams and swim lanes

I described how to create spaghetti diagrams and swim lanes in Chapter 3. These provide visual representations of potentially wasted transport or motion.

With physical transport or motion, it is possible to calculate the actual distances travelled and so gain a very concrete idea of how much saving might be possible. Clients have used data from spaghetti diagrams to make a case to management for a different design of their working area.

With virtual processes, spaghetti diagrams can provide a graphic illustration when making a case for reducing the number of people who have to sign off or be consulted in a process.

Figures 4.4 and 4.5 are illustrations from Scenarios 1 and 2 respectively.

29

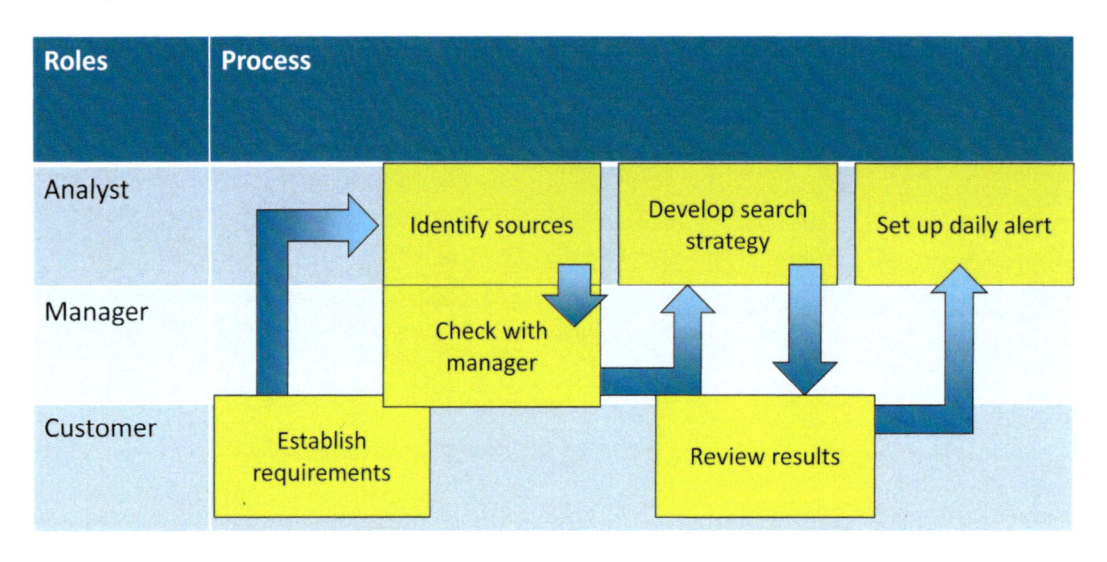

Figure 4.4 Swim lane representation of Scenario 1

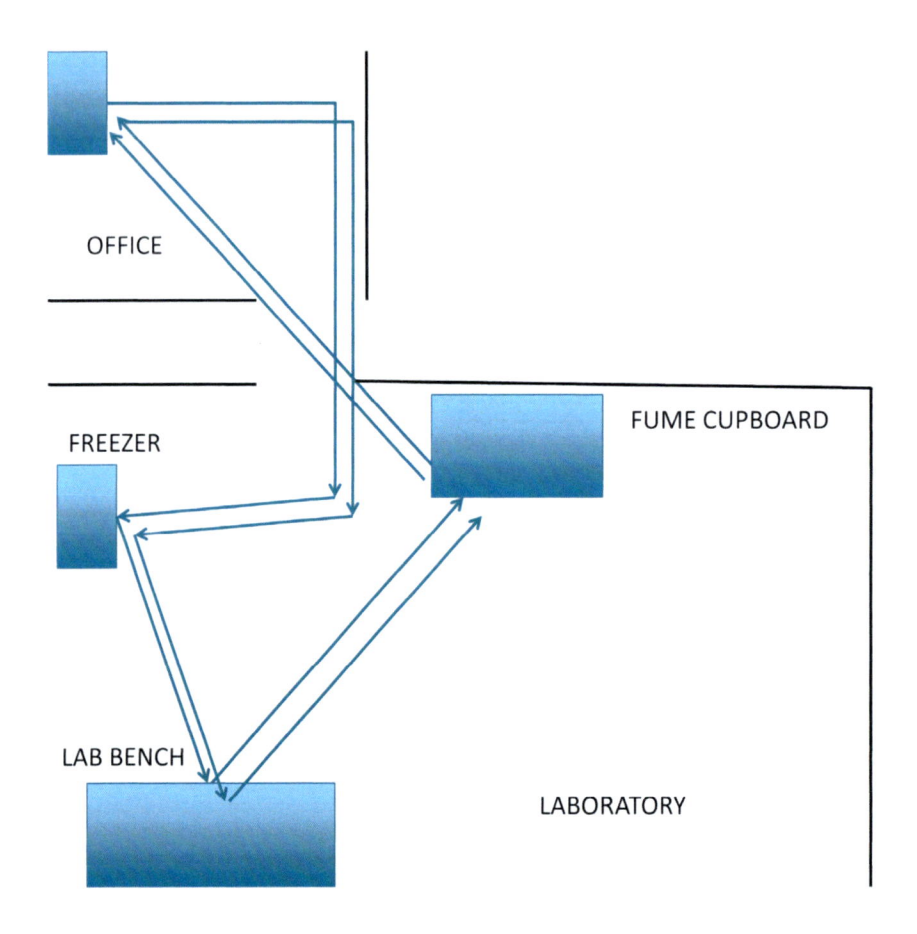

Figure 4.5 Spaghetti diagram of Scenario 2

Wastes

It should be obvious by now that there are several different ways of wasting time, money and the talents of individuals within the team. Taiichi Ohno identified several definitions of waste as part of the Toyota Production System, and these can be applied to any field of endeavour. I typically use eight definitions of waste, as shown in Table 4.1, although I have seen others use variations of up to ten of these. Each of these wastes can be identified using a range of tools, several of which have already been described in this and the previous chapter.

Type of waste	Potential Problem
Defects	Quality that does not meet customer requirements
Inventory	Products or services (including work in progress) piling up prior to use
Processing	More work than is needed e.g. for review or to meet customer needs
Overproduction	Delivery is too fast or there is too much product / service for needs
Motion	Unnecessary movement of individuals during production
Transport	Unnecessary 'transport' during production (go for cellular layout)
Waiting	Waiting between steps for things to happen (batching vs. one-piece flow)
Creativity	Staff creativity / potential not being used

Table 4.1 Ohno's wastes help to identify issues with time, cost or quality

Defects. If the quality of the product or service does not meet customer requirements then the work will have to be redone resulting in wasted time and cost. Ideally, there should be ways to monitor quality and take corrective action during the process, rather than waiting until the product or service is complete.

Inventory. Raw and intermediate materials, final products and services take up space and storage space can be costly. Materials could also be expensive to replace if they are time-sensitive and stay as inventory beyond their lifespan.

Processing. We or our managers may think more work is needed on a product or service than is actually the case. This may be because we do not know quite what is needed, or because we are perfectionists! At any rate, knowing when to stop could save time and resources.

Overproduction. If more product is generated than the customer wants, then this is a potential waste. For a service this could mean generating more information that is needed. The extra time or cost involved are obviously wasted in this situation.

Overproduction could also involve intermediates, final products or services being delivered faster than this is required by 'little c' or 'big C' customers. Although this might look good in terms of internal performance metrics, it is not a Lean way of responding to customer "pull". The possible consequence is that materials or information go out of date before they are used, take up valuable space that could be used for other purposes, or use time and resources that might be better spent on other priorities.

Motion and transport are wasted whenever the flow of work in a physical environment or of information between people or departments is not streamlined. This results in excessive to-ing and fro-ing, and consequent time wastage. This is where the spaghetti diagram and swim lane representations can help you to detect and quantify the waste.

Waiting is perhaps the most obvious type of waste but sometimes the hardest to address as it often requires influencing others to work differently so that they are not acting as bottlenecks in the process. It may also be caused by having to wait for equipment, materials etc. Again, quantifying the extent of the delay will make it easier to demonstrate the impact that it is having on the process and so influence others to help streamline it.

Waiting can also be caused by our tendency to go for batch processing rather than 'single piece' flow. Batch processing is traditionally deemed more efficient in terms of the use of our resources. But if this introduces a delay relative to the customer's preferred delivery time then the outcome is not effective.

The time-value map will help to show up waiting time.

Creativity. Our tendency to put up with wasted time and effort, and to fire-fight rather than plan and prevent problems, results in lost opportunities for making the most of people's talents. True they can, and often do, apply their skills to fire-fighting, but their talents would be put to much better use if given the time for continuous improvement, or even breakthrough innovation or 'blue sky' thinking.

A mind-set and culture of continuous improvement will enable people to use their talents, and also create more space and time for innovation.

Illustrations from the scenarios

Scenario 1

Defects – there are no obvious defects to be found from the data shown in this workbook. The most likely sources of error are if the customer requirements have not been fully understood, if the sources selected have been incomplete or incorrect, and if insufficient or incorrect information has been included in the search strategy.

Inventory, Processing, Overproduction – these do not appear to be an issue.

Motion, Transport – the swim lane representation in Figure 4.4 does suggest some waste is involved in checking sources with the manager; see the comment about this under creativity. The amount of to-ing and fro-ing with the customer is probably already the minimum required to ensure the quality of the final deliverable.

Waiting – one hour between establishing requirements and looking for sources; 45 minutes waiting for the manager to check that the right sources have been selected; 20 minutes waiting to review the results and strategy with the customer; 20 minutes before the daily alert is set up.

Creativity – the various stoppages caused by the waiting delays may mean that the analyst has to refresh his / her memory each time about where he or she has got to, so that they will not be making the most productive use of their time. The need to check with their manager that they have selected the right sources may be appropriate to their stage of professional development, but this step should be reviewed periodically to ensure that it is still appropriate.

Scenario 2

Defects – again there are no obvious defects to be found from the data collected.

Inventory – there is an issue here in that the required reagents were not available and so had to be ordered, thereby introducing delays in the overall process.

Processing, Overproduction – these do not appear to be an issue.

Motion, Transport – the spaghetti diagram in Figure 4.5 is relatively sparse, so that it may seem that little streamlining is needed. However the need to physically walk around to check on supplies of reagents and conditions of the fume cupboard could be seen as wasted movement, as also suggested by the time-value map in Figure 4.3.

Waiting – there were small delays between receiving customer requirements and accessing the SOP, and also between completing the test and writing it up. Figure 4.3 shows that there were more significant delays in waiting for reagents that had to be ordered (24 hours), checking the correct SOP with the customer (2 hours).

Creativity – there are definite opportunities for streamlining the process, as suggested by the time-value map. The time saved, if used well, could allow the individual to spend more time on other things such as professional development or innovation.

Finding the root causes

Whether it is an urban myth or a true account, this version of the Jefferson Memorial building story (Figure 4.6) is the one that I share with my workshop delegates to help them appreciate why the obvious solution to a problem is not necessarily the right one, and why it is important to look for the root cause or causes. (There is some research on the origins of the '5 whys folklore' in the Further Reading section.)

Figure 4.6 An image of the Jefferson Memorial Building

This is how the story goes:

"A beautiful white building was suffering from the effects of too many birds and their droppings, incurring costs and time for repeated cleaning. Rather than take the obvious but not politically acceptable solution to the problem (shooting the birds), someone asked WHY there were so many birds. The answer was that there were lots of spiders, and the birds were eating the spiders. Same thing for the reason WHY there were so many spiders: lots of midges.

The obvious solution would have been to use insecticides. However they went further and asked WHY there were so many midges. It seemed that the midges were being attracted when the outside lights were switched on at dusk.

Someone had the idea of delaying the timing for switching on the lights by one hour... this resulted in a drop in the midge, spider and bird populations and so less bird droppings and less cost and time for cleaning. An additional benefit was a saving in electricity."

The 5 Why's. This is the simplest way of finding root causes, as demonstrated by the Jefferson Memorial Building story and illustrated in Figure 4.7

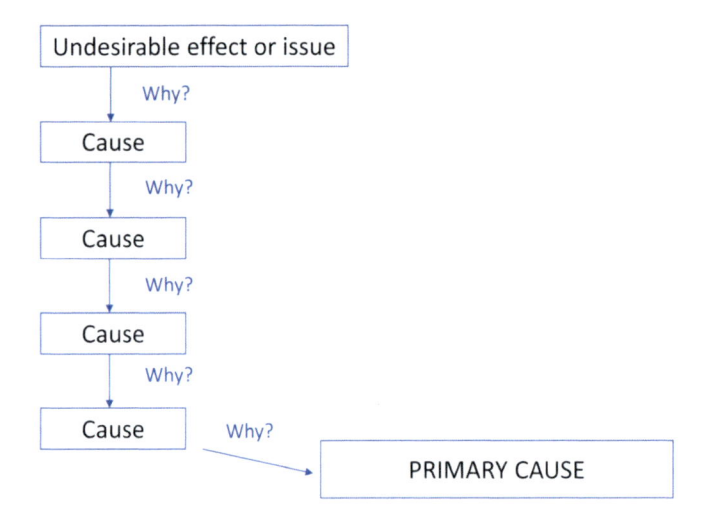

Figure 4.7 The 5 Why's

It is important to start by clearly articulating the issue being analysed and, if possible, to do so in a way that is quantified, typically in terms of wasted time, cost or quality. To say something is of poor quality, takes too long, or costs too much is too subjective. Objective or quantified statements would be for example:

a. We are having to repeat this particular step on average two or three times
b. This step is taking up to three days when it should take less than a day
c. We are having to spend £50 more on this than we would expect

You then ask: 'why is this happening' between four to six times until it becomes futile to question any further.

Unlike the example we used in the urban myth story, the answer to the question 'why' can be more than one at any stage.

Figure 4.8 shows an illustration from Scenario 2.

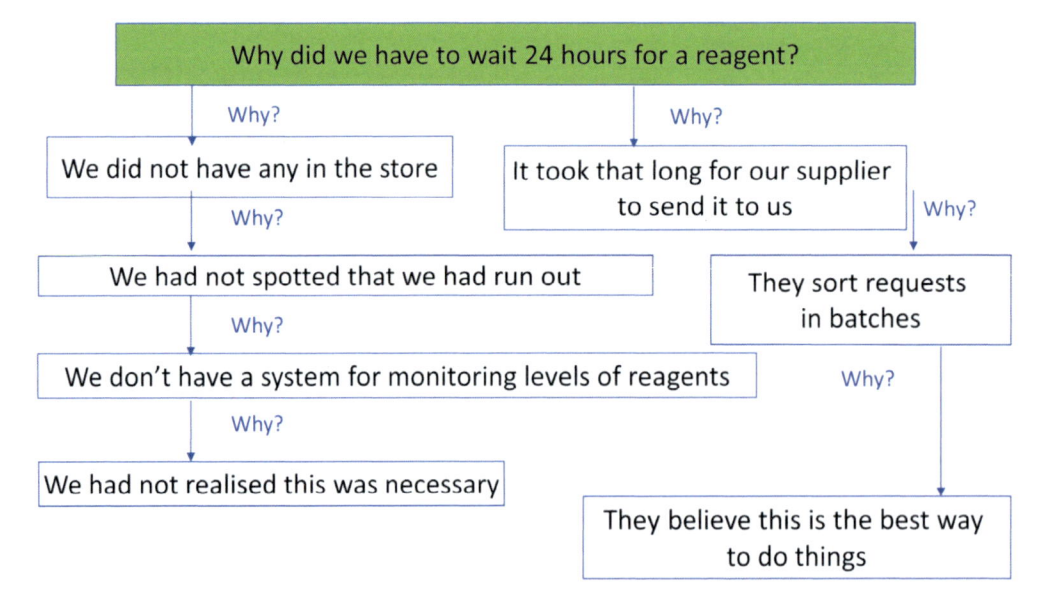

Figure 4.8 An illustration of the 5 Why's from Scenario 2

Fishbone analysis. Whilst a lot of people like the 5 Why's analysis for its simplicity, its open-ended approach can also result in key root causes being missed. The fishbone analysis (Figure 4.9), so named because it resembles a fish skeleton, provides a more structured approach that can often yield additional root causes.

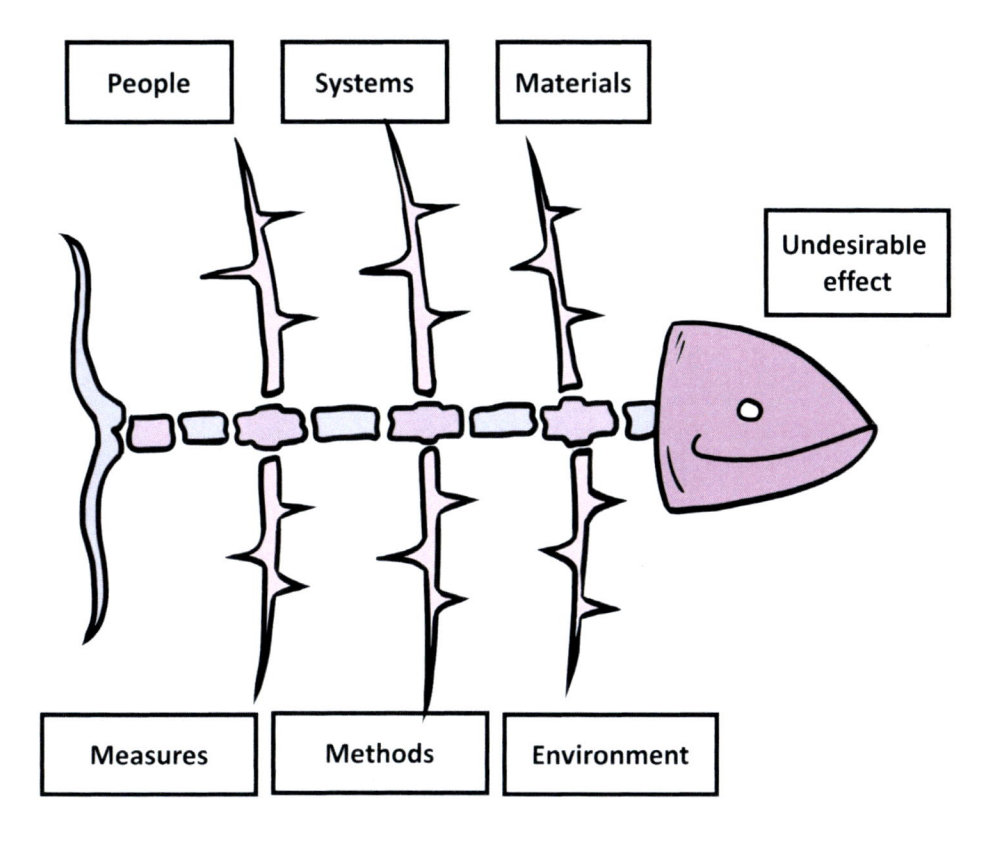

Figure 4.9 Fishbone analysis

Each of the headings acts as a prompt to tease out potential root causes. There are different versions of these headings around, but the ones shown work well for my students. The important thing is to use them as prompts only, and not to worry if it is not obvious which heading a particular cause sits under, if it sits under more than one, or if indeed none can be found for a heading.

Figure 4.10 is an illustration of the Fishbone analysis for the same issue as that found for Scenario 2 with the 5 Why's. The analysis shows one additional root cause to those found in the 5 Why's and it is likely that a group discussion would reveal several more.

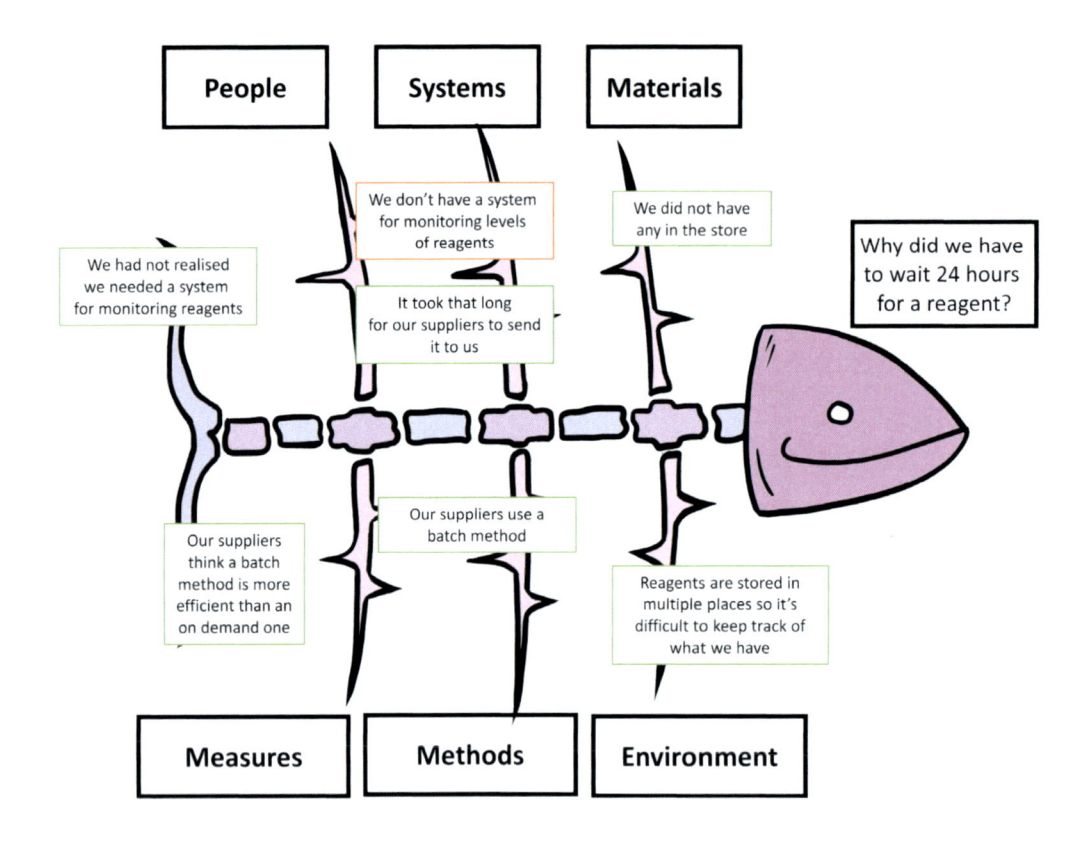

Figure 4.10 An illustration of the Fishbone analysis for Scenario 2

Team exercise 4.1 Analyse your data

Step 1. Visualise your data.

With your team, and using the data that you collected in Chapter 3, represent your process in as many ways as possible:

   a. A process flow
   b. A time-value map
   c. A spaghetti diagram
   d. A swim-lane diagram

Step 2. Find your wastes.

Uses Ohno's categories of wastes as prompts to interrogate your visual representations and find as many wastes as possible. Make sure you describe them in quantified terms based on time, cost or quality. You may not find examples of all the wastes, and some that you do find may fall under more than one category. Again, it is not the categorisation that is important so much as the ability to find the wastes.

Step 3. Identify the root causes

Choose the wastes that are having the biggest impact on your effectiveness or efficiency, and use the 5 Why's and the Fishbone analysis to find as many root causes as possible. You will use these as the basis for identifying solutions in the next chapter.

Closing thoughts

There are several other tools, such as interrelationship diagrams, Pareto analysis, and various matrices that can be used to help evaluate and prioritise issues and root causes.

Although I do offer longer, more in-depth "expert practitioner" Lean and Six Sigma training, the workshop that this book is based upon typically runs for only one day, so that there is not time to cover these additional tools. Instead participants use a combination of individual intuition and discussion within their working groups to identify the issues and root causes to take forward. I ask you to take a similar approach here. But if you would like to find out more about these other tools and how to use them, do get in touch with me, or take a look at Bicheno, or at Morgan and Brenig-Jones in the Further Reading section.

Lastly, I would also like to make a brief reference to Appreciative Enquiry. The focus of Lean and Six Sigma is very much on picking out issues and how to address them. In this book I have also mentioned the value of identifying good practices, and exploring ways of adopting them more widely. This is the spirit of Appreciative Enquiry: to look for successes and opportunities to repeat them.

You could if you wish experiment with this idea during the Measure and Analyse phases: find examples of what is working particularly well, and then explore the root causes for these successes. This should then give you ideas for how to repeat and extend good practices across your processes and teams.

I have included a reference by Hammond on Appreciative Enquiry at the end of the book.

Chapter 5. Exploring the Solutions

"Let your imagination soar"

Background and principles

This chapter addresses the Improve step in the DMAIC sequence. Critiques of Lean and Six Sigma sometimes complain that its structured approach blocks creativity. On the contrary, the use of data and root cause analysis provides lots of opportunity to be creative and find opportunities for improvement. Whilst this may be incremental rather than breakthrough innovation, it is possible to bring in 'blue sky' thinking too.

Participants in my workshops who aspire to 'blue sky' thinking sometimes do this by forming a break away group from the rest of the discussion. They start with a fresh sheet of paper and design a new 'to be' process, whilst their colleagues explore step-by-step solutions for the root causes to come up with their version of an improved process. Comparison of the two outcomes provokes useful and productive discussion.

Whether you start with 'blue sky' thinking, or adopt more incremental continuous improvement, the important thing is to allow as much 'divergent' thinking as possible to come up with the new ideas, before evaluating them and so 'converging' to preferred solutions that can be recommended to management or implemented straight-a-way.

Coming up with the solutions

The Six Thinking Hats. There are many brainstorming techniques that can be used to generate ideas, and which ones you use can be influenced by how much time you have, the nature of the group (the mix of extroverts / introverts, their comfort with each other), as well as personal preferences.

Edward de Bono is a well-known writer in the field of all types of thinking, and I used his 'Six Thinking Hats' in "The Effective Team's High Performance Workbook" as an approach to support divergent and then convergent thinking.

> "The hats are metaphors for a particular way of thinking. Each colour hat is 'worn' by all participants in the discussion at the same time, to ensure that everyone can have their say, and that ideas are not dismissed too soon. The order in which the colours are to be worn can be agreed at the start of the discussion."

I have reproduced the original illustration in figure 5.1.

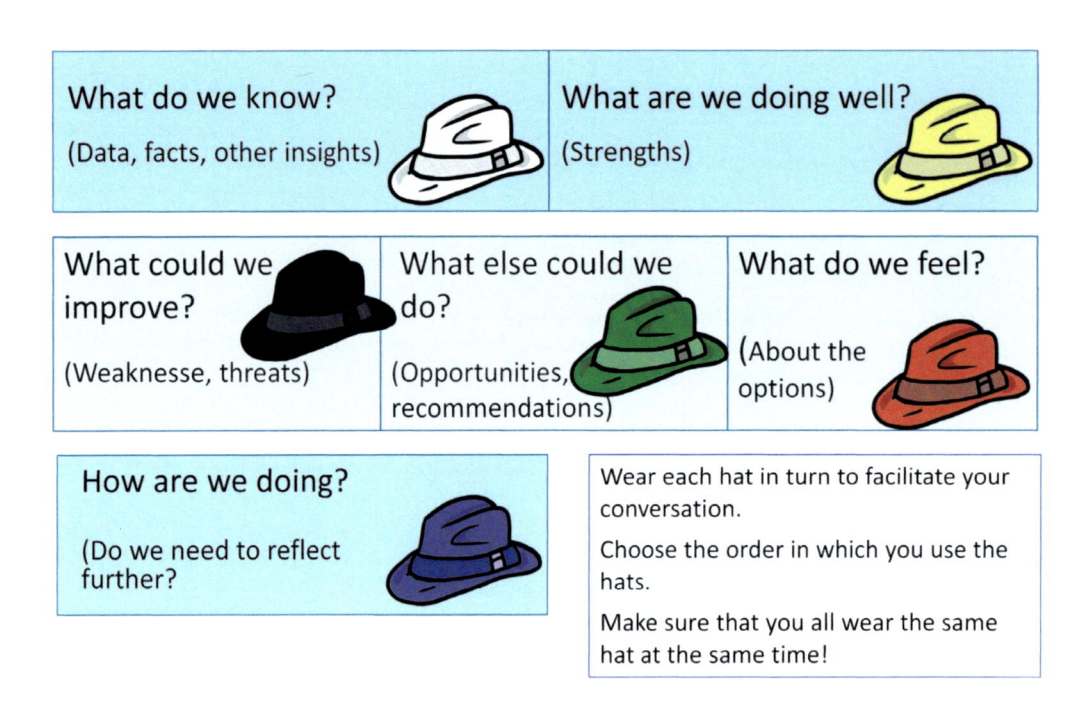

Figure 5.1 Edward de Bono's 'Six Thinking Hats', from "The Effective Team's High Performance Workbook", RiverRhee Publishing, 2014.

Using the 'Six Thinking Hats' for the Improve phase of DMAIC goes something like this (note the order can be changed to suit different purposes):

a. The **white** hat is about reviewing all of the data that you have collected and analysed so far. You use it to agree which wastes and root causes you would like to focus on. (There's a little bit of blue hat thinking going on here too to direct the discussion).
b. The **green** hat is used to generate all of the possible solutions for addressing the wastes and root causes. It is important to allow as much time as possible for generating ideas, so that you may come up with apparently extraordinary ideas. Keep reviewing the root causes as prompts for more possibilities. People often find that it is the last ideas that are the ones chosen for implementation. All of the ideas are typically captured on a flip chart.
c. Each idea is then evaluated, using the **yellow** (pros) and **black** (cons) hats in turn.
d. People then use the **red** hat to express how they feel about each idea having gone through the pros and cons.
e. The **blue** hat is used last to evaluate the outcome and check whether further reflection is needed, and if so with which hats.

Illustrations from the scenarios

One of the wastes that we found in Scenario 2 was in having to wait 24 hours for materials from a supplier due to their use of batch processing for deliveries. This is a common issue in all sorts of businesses and sectors, so I will use it to illustrate the use of the Six Thinking Hats.

White	Green	Yellow	Black	Red	Blue
24 hour wait for supplies due to batch processing by supplier who believes this is the most efficient way of doing things	1. Meet with supplier to explain needs	Discussion key to an effective partnership	May not be very receptive	+++	We have several options (1-4) that we can explore at this stage, and an alternative (5) if the other options do not work out.
	2. Explain how batch processing is not the most effective for the client	Ditto	Ditto	+++	
	3. Research and tell them about alternative approaches used by other suppliers	Evidence may increase receptiveness	Will take time to do this. May not find what we are looking for	+++	
	4. Partner with other companies who use same supplier	Could offer efficiency alternative to supplier. Gives us more weight to influence	Not enough similar companies in area. Competition	++	
	5. Use a different supplier	Will work if we can find the right one	Costly to change. May not find	- (only explore if other options don't work out)	
	6. Merge with/ acquire a supplier	Gives us control. May offer other opportunities for business development	Costly. Risky. May not suit business model. Will take time	_ _ (not appropriate for current status of business)	
	Etc.				

Table 5.1 Using the Six Thinking Hats on one of the issues from Scenario 2

Some people like to use smiley, neutral, or sad faces in the red hat column to indicate their level of enthusiasm for each solution.

41

Using matrices to evaluate solutions.

Although the yellow, black and red hats provide a method for evaluating the solutions, people have also found it useful to use one or more matrices as shown in Figures 5.2 and 5.3.

The **4-box matrix** (or 'Boston Square') in Figure 5.2 is a relatively simple visual that helps to identify 'quick wins', and potential longer-term projects. I have used it with teams to present recommendations to senior managers, who sometimes like to revisit the positioning of the solutions in the various boxes! This is a great way to obtain their engagement and buy-in for the final approach.

The 4-box matrix compares solutions against just 2 criteria: ease of implementation and business impact.

The 4-box approach is a simpler version of the evaluation matrix

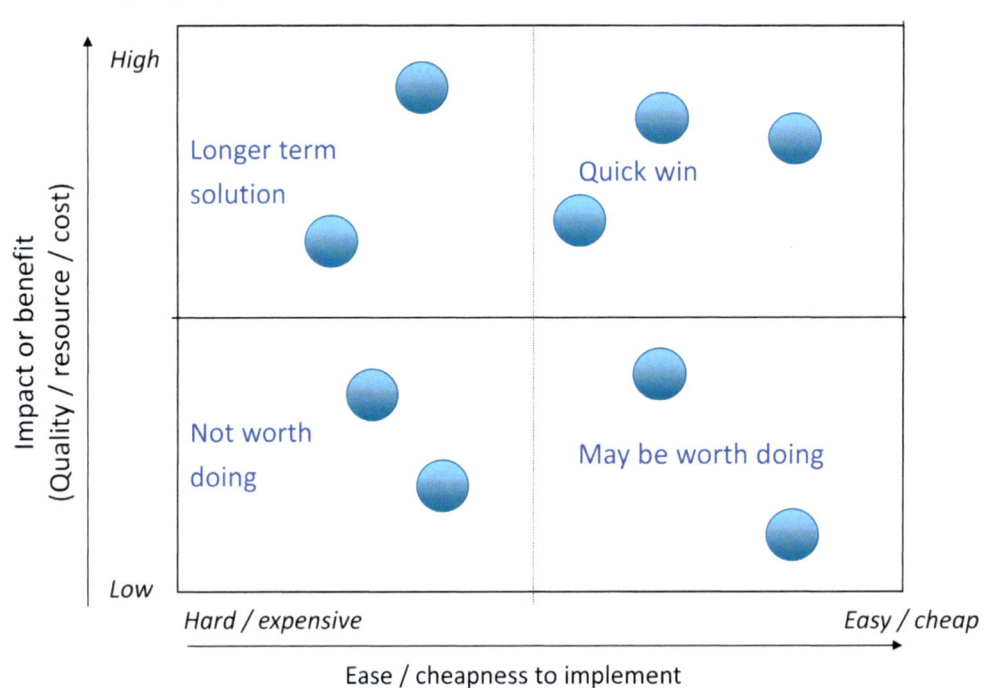

Figure 5.2 The 4-box matrix for evaluating solutions

More **complex matrices**, such as the one shown in Figure 5.3, enable the group to add other criteria such as price. It is important when using such matrices to agree on the criteria that will be used, and how the scoring will be applied. It is not unusual for a group to complete the exercise and decide that they want to make a different choice to the one that the scoring has revealed. If this happens, the group has at least had the opportunity to air their views and to understand why they are making a particular choice. The tool is simply one to facilitate the discussion, whatever the outcome.

Solution	Controls the problem	Easy to do	Good price	Strategic impact	Total
A	1	2	3	2	8
B	1	3	1	1	6
C	2	1	1	3	7
D	2	1	3	1	7

Criteria for evaluating the solutions

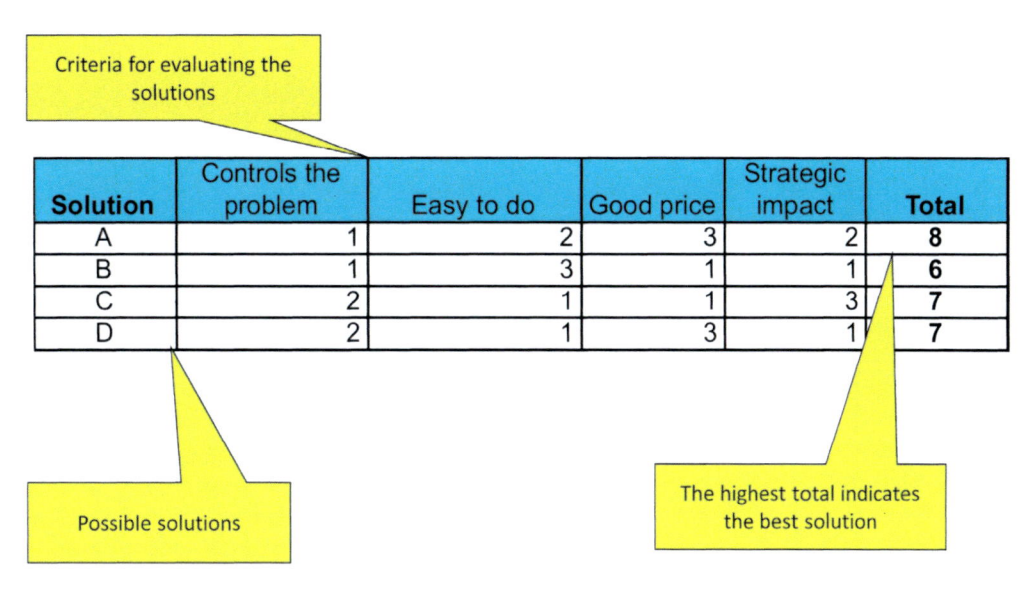

Possible solutions

The highest total indicates the best solution

Figure 5.3 An alternative, complex, matrix for evaluating solutions

Illustrations from the scenarios

Figure 5.4 shows how the 4-box matrix would come out if completed for the six solutions identified with the Six Thinking Hats for Scenario 2.

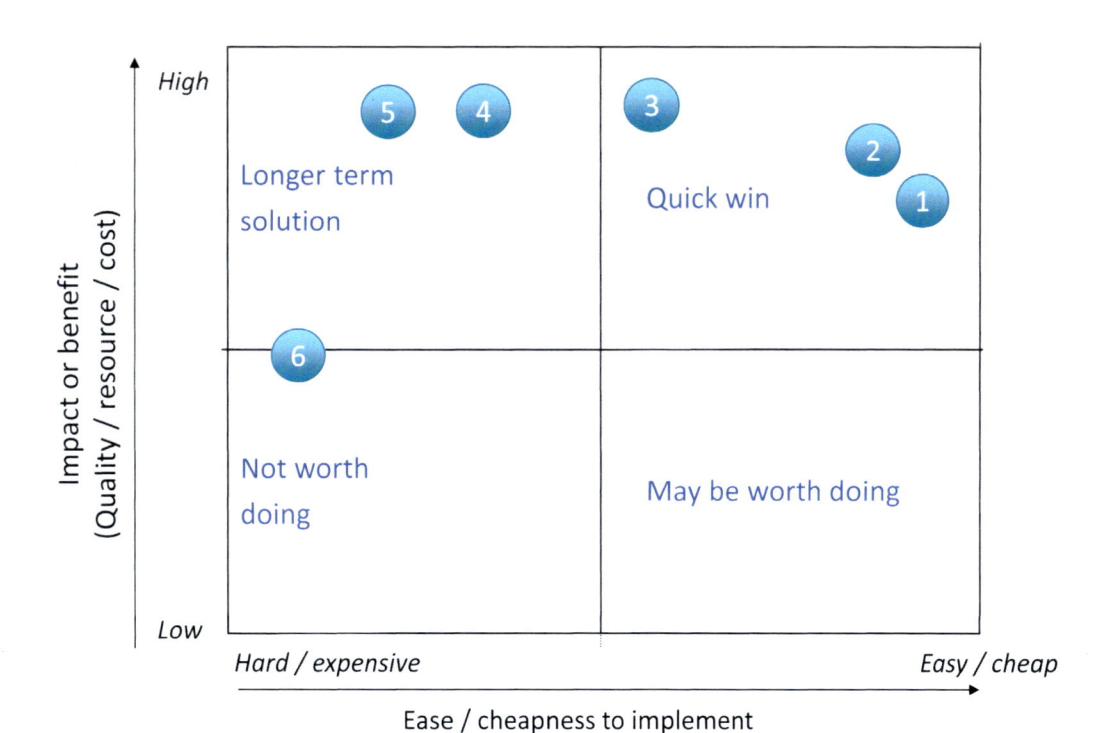

Figure 5.4 A 4-box matrix completed for the solutions identified in Table 5.1 for Scenario 2

43

Table 5.2 shows the more detailed evaluation of the same solutions, with the more complex matrix.

Solution	Controls the problem	Easy to do	Good price	Strategic impact	Total
1	1	3	3	2	9
2	2	3	3	2	10
3	3	2	3	3	11
4	3	1	2	2	8
5	3	1	1	3	8
6	3	1	1	2	7

Table 5.2 Complex matrix completed for the solutions identified in Table 5.1 for Scenario 2

Team exercise 5.1 Identify and evaluate solutions

Step 1. Select the root causes.

Identify the most important root causes for your process

Step 2. Try out the Six Thinking Hats to brainstorm some solutions.

Step 3. Evaluate the solutions.

Use the 4-box matrix and/or complex matrix to evaluate your solutions

Step 4. Double-check the final solutions.

Look back at your original wastes to help you assess how well the solutions you select will address the time, cost and quality issues with your process.

Planning for implementation

Your solutions are likely to involve or otherwise affect any number of people including the colleagues within your team or in another parts of the organisation, suppliers or customers. Ideally you will have involved or alerted them in some way as part of your operational excellence programme. Even if you have not involved them yet, they may have some valuable input for you to consider before you implement new tools, methods or other factors that will affect your and their work.

My earlier book "The Effective Team's Change Management Workbook" contains a step-by-step approach for managing change. Here are a few extracts of the principles and tools to be aware of:

1. **Change is a personal journey.**
   Two people may react to any given change in a very different way. It will depend on a whole mix of things including their previous experiences of change and what else is going on in their home and work lives at the moment. They may perceive the change as something positive, or negative. Either way, they are likely to experience both ups and downs.
2. **Resistance is useful!**
   Many people implementing change get anxious if they experience resistance, but actually it is something to be welcomed: it provides valuable information that you can work from – by improving your solutions, improving your communication, or making what may be difficult decisions about anyone who absolutely refuses to change. The important thing is to engage in two-way dialogue with the people affected so that you can understand their perspective and respond accordingly.

3. Consider each of the people affected by the change as your 'stakeholders' and plan for implementation accordingly.

Successful change relies on understanding and influencing attitudes, skills and behaviour. Each of your stakeholders or stakeholder groups needs to be considered within this context.

Team exercise 5.2 Plan for implementation

Step 1. Identify your stakeholders.

Think about all the people who might be affected in some way, or have a role to play in helping you to implement your solution or solutions.

Step 2. Analyse your stakeholders.

Jot down some notes on your perception of each of your stakeholders' likely attitude and/or skill sets in relation to the proposed solutions, and what attitude and/or skills they would need to take the solutions on board. You may need to talk to them to better understand their perspectives!

Step 3. Plan your influencing approaches.

Put together some ideas for how you might influence your stakeholders or help them to bridge the gap between where they are now and where they need to be. Methods used could be one-to-one conversations and other forms of verbal communication, written communication, training, on-line support etc.

Closing thoughts

Your 'solution' might have involved doing some blue sky thinking to come up with an alternative 'to be' process to replace your current 'as is' process.

A good practice, when coming up with your new 'to be' process, or indeed when planning for the implementation of any of your solutions, is to carry out some risk analysis of the new way of working.

FMEA (or failure mode effect analysis) is a particularly useful tool for this, as shown in Figure 5.6, with an example filled in for solution 4 in Scenario 2: partnering with other companies to influence the practices of a supplier.

FMEA is a way of assessing all of the things that might go wrong in a particular process or solution, evaluating those potential 'failures', prioritising them, and identifying actions to take to prevent them happening or to alleviate them if they do.

What might go wrong	Likelihood	Impact	Control measures in place?	LxIxC	Mitigation plans
Not enough suitable local companies	5	10	3	150	Define what is 'enough'. It may be that just one or two partners will be sufficient
Confidentiality risk	6	9	3	162	Start with the supply of standard materials that everyone would use, and then assess risk with others
Supplier will not be influenced	3	10	6	180	Have early conversation to establish general willingness to explore options for improving quality of service. If not interested consider approaching other suppliers.

Table 5.3 Failure mode effect analysis (FMEA) – an illustration for 'partnering with other companies to influence a supplier'

The scales for Likelihood, Impact and Control Measures can be from 1-10 or some other range. In this case, 1 is lowest and 10 is highest. Note that 'Control' is an inverse scale so that if the risk is easy to detect, or there are control measures in place, then the score will be low. The definition for each point on the scales should be agreed within the team.

You might like to try out this tool for your own solutions. A template is available at the end of the book.

Chapter 6. What Happens Next?

"If you're not measuring it you can't manage it"

Background and principles

In Chapter 3 I introduced the value of measurement to help clarify targets for performance for operational excellence and to identify where performance is falling short of those targets so that something can be done about it.

The Control phase of DMAIC is about putting measurements in place to determine whether the benefits anticipated from the solutions are being realised, and to also continue to monitor performance and fresh opportunities for improvement.

In Chapter 2 I also introduced the different criteria that customers might specify in terms of the quality of your product or service. When you select the criteria to measure your performance against, you might want to consider how you could monitor your work as it is progressing (also known as in-process or lead measures), rather than waiting until it is complete (outcome or lag measures).

As the term 'lag' measure implies, it will give you historical information, whereas, had you been monitoring the 'lead' measure, you might have been able to take corrective action sooner and thereby saved on time, money and other resources.

Control charts

The volume of product or service being produced may be such that you can use control charts to monitor performance against specific criteria such as time, cost or quality, as shown in Figure 6.1.

Control charts require setting upper and lower control limits for the expected performance, together with taking measurements at appropriate and regular intervals. Known causes may temporarily affect performance. Significant shifts in performance would have to be investigated. New downward or upward trends may result in the control limits being reassessed.

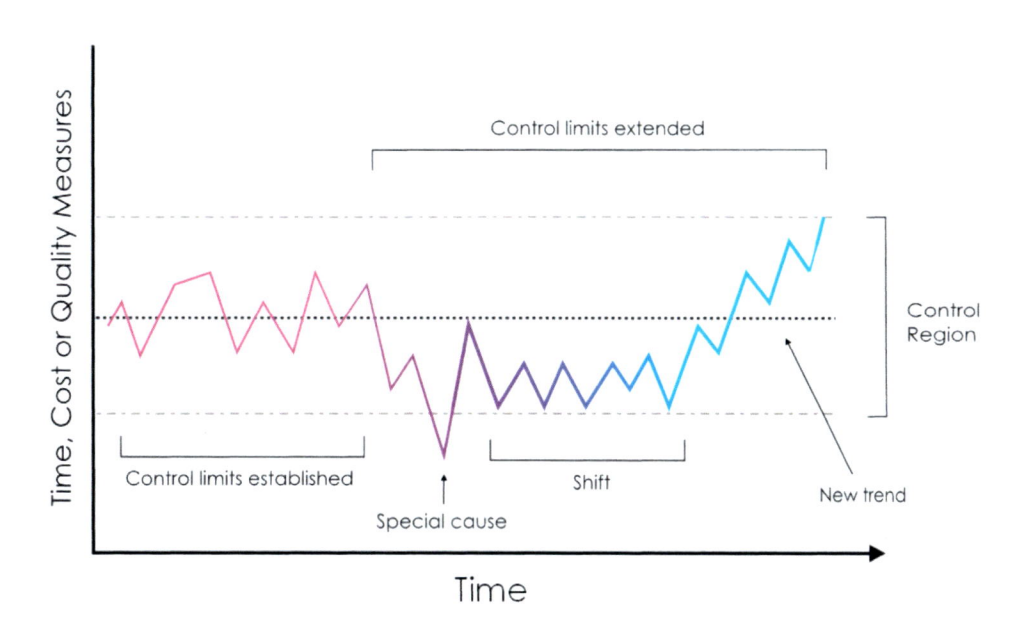

Figure 6.1 Example of a control chart

'Fail safe' approaches

Having staff whose sole role is to control the quality of your work, whether as you are doing it, or at the final stage, is another potentially non-value adding overhead! The ideal is to get things right first time so that there is no need to have someone dedicated to checking quality, and no need to redo work for defective products or services.

'Fail safe' approaches do just that. Examples are shown in Figure 6.2 and include the UK 3-pin plug where it is only possible to insert a plug one way; Excel spreadsheets where data must be selected from a choice on a drop-down list; machines that stop when the operating lever is released.

Figure 6.2 Examples of 'fail safe' approaches

Team exercise 6.1 What measures would be useful for you?

Consider the following questions:

1. What measures do you already have in place, and what new / improved ones would be useful for the processes and solutions that you explored?
2. Do you have any existing measures that are superfluous?
3. What 'fail safe' approaches could you use?
4. How will you know that your anticipated benefits are being realised and that you are working towards operational excellence?
5. What would prompt you to begin another cycle of continuous improvement?

Concluding thoughts

You should now be well on your way to achieving operational excellence. Remember that it is a continuous process, and the Control phase of DMAIC will help you to monitor and identify those further opportunities for improvement.

I have already mentioned the existing workbook on change management, as one to help you with the implementation of your improvements. You may find some of the other available and planned books in this series helpful too.

- "The Effective Team's Change Management Workbook" (published November 2013, ISBN 978-0-9926323-5-9) will help you to appreciate personal journeys, reactions and resistance to change and the processes to use when planning and implementing various types of change.
- "The Effective Team's High Performance Workbook" (published August 2014, ISBN 978-0-9926323-6-6) will help you to explore the team development journey, tools for valuing the individual, defining the team's purpose and goals, self-evaluation of the team, and developing good working practices.
- "The Effective Team's Knowledge Management Workbook" will help you to make the most of the knowledge and expertise available within your team, and from others that you work with.
- Finally, "The Effective Team's Facilitation Workbook" will give you tools and techniques for stimulating your team's creativity in one-off exercises, half and one-day workshops, or when engaged in projects.

I would be very interested to hear of any feedback or questions that you may have on any aspect of enhancing team effectiveness.

Please get in touch at publishing@riverrhee.com

Six Sigma

My approach to operational excellence weaves many of the Lean and Six Sigma concepts together. The statistical basis of Six Sigma is essential for defining and monitoring quality, and reducing variation. It is not something that my clients are generally interested in at the point where I am working with them. So I am including a brief synopsis here for those who are interested. There is obviously a lot more to this should you wish to find out more about it.

Six Sigma is about reducing variation so as to deliver the quality expected by the customer. Every object, product or service will have variation. To understand this variation, we need to be able to measure it. We could measure a very obvious physical attribute, such as size or weight, or something perhaps less obvious such as timeliness or completeness of information.

There are two essential components for measuring and establishing Six Sigma: the voice of the customer, and the voice of the process, as shown in Figure 1.

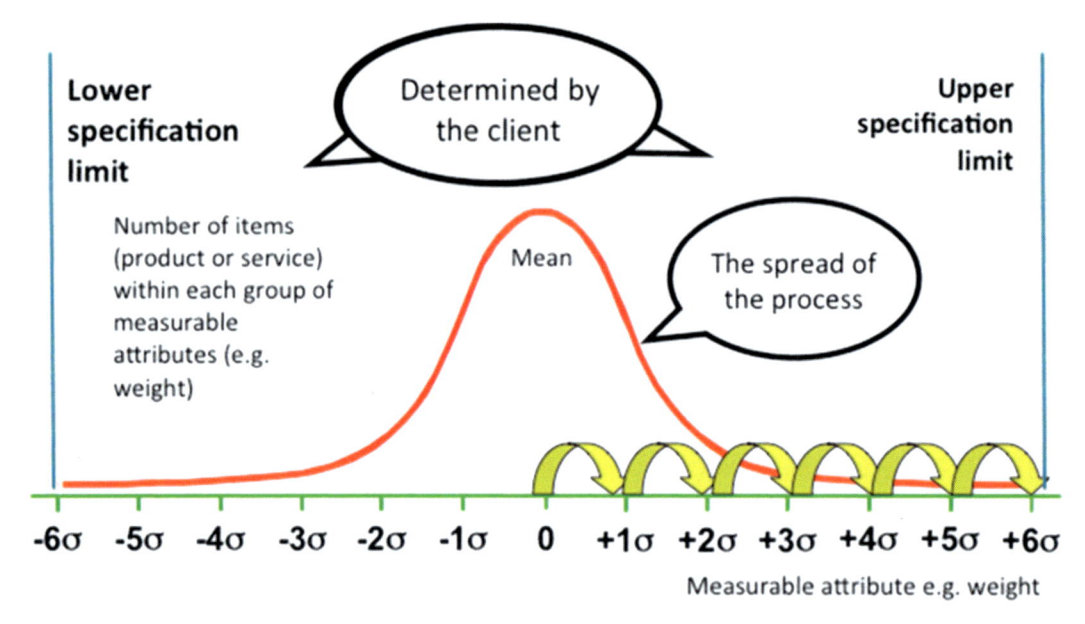

Sigma capability is the number of standard deviations (or sigmas) on either side of the mean before reaching the limits set by the client

Figure 1. Process chart showing variation in resultant products / services

The process in Figure 1 is a Six Sigma one: all six variations on either side of the mean in the resultant product or service fall within the lower and upper specifications set by the client.

Figure 2 shows a three sigma process. This time only three variations on either side of the mean fall within the limits set by the customer. The customer has defined a much tighter specification, and the process will need to be improved in order to be able to consistently deliver within it. Only by improving the process will all six sigmas of variation be able to fall within the specified limits.

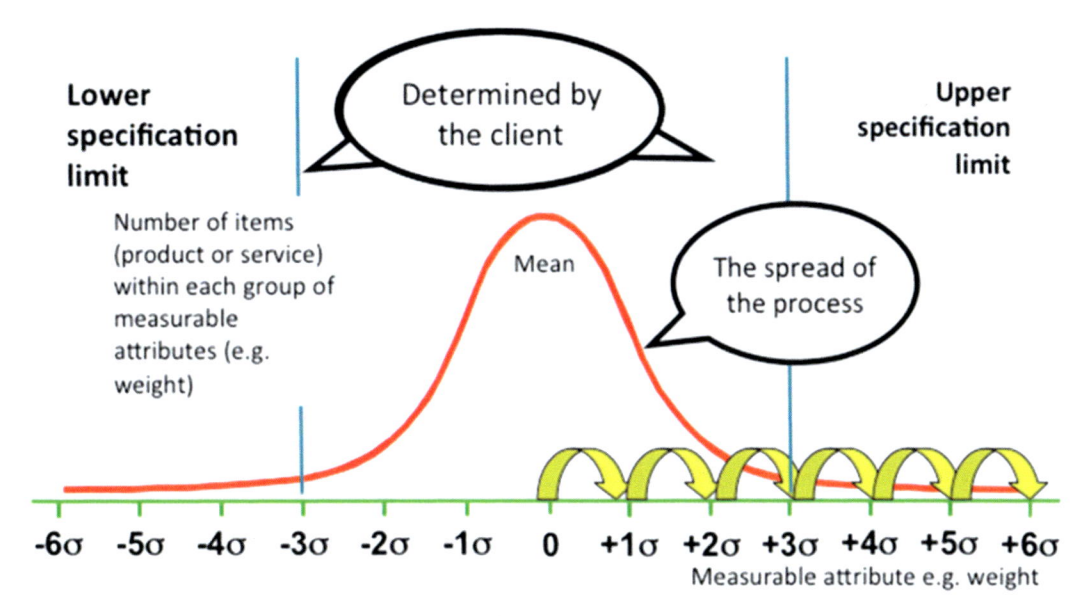

Figure 2. A three sigma process

Six Sigma has been selected as a norm because of the relative impact that this has been shown to have as illustrated by the data in Table 1. (These data were shared with me when I was learning about Lean and Six Sigma.)

99% success (3.8 Sigma)	99.99966% success (6 Sigma)
20,000 items of post lost per hour	7 items of post lost per hour
Undrinkable water for 15 minutes per day	One minute of undrinkable water every 7 months
5,000 surgical errors per week	1.7 errors per week
Two landings falling too short or too far at all major airports per day	One landing too short / far every 5 years
200,000 prescription errors per year	68 prescription errors per year
No electricity for nearly 7 hours per month	No electricity one hour every 34 years

Table 1. Why Six Sigma? (Comparative data.)

Full Page Versions of Materials for Use in Workshops

Suppliers	Inputs	Process	Outputs	Customers

FINISH ← → START

Adapted from Figure 2.3 The SIPOC framework for improving an area of work

Taken from Chapter 2 Working with your Customers – in "The Effective Team's Operational Excellence Workbook", RiverRhee Publishing, 2015

Step	Description	Start time	End time	Total time	Delay

Adapted from Table 3.1 A timesheet for collecting data on a process

Taken from Chapter 3 – Gathering Data – in "The Effective Team's Operational Excellence Workbook", RiverRhee Publishing, 2015

Step	Process	Activity	Start time	End time	Total time	Delay

Adapted from Table 3.2 A timesheet for collecting data on all of an individual's or team's activities

Taken from Chapter 3 – Gathering Data – in "The Effective Team's Operational Excellence Workbook", RiverRhee Publishing, 2015

Step	Activity	Distance	Start time	End time	Total time	Delay

Adapted from Table 3.3 A timesheet with column for physical motion data

Taken from Chapter 3 – Gathering Data – in "The Effective Team's Operational Excellence Workbook", RiverRhee Publishing, 2015

Step	Description	From / To	Start time	End time	Total time	Delay

Adapted from Table 3.4 A timesheet with column for virtual motion data

Taken from Chapter 3 – Gathering Data – in "The Effective Team's Operational Excellence Workbook", RiverRhee Publishing, 2015

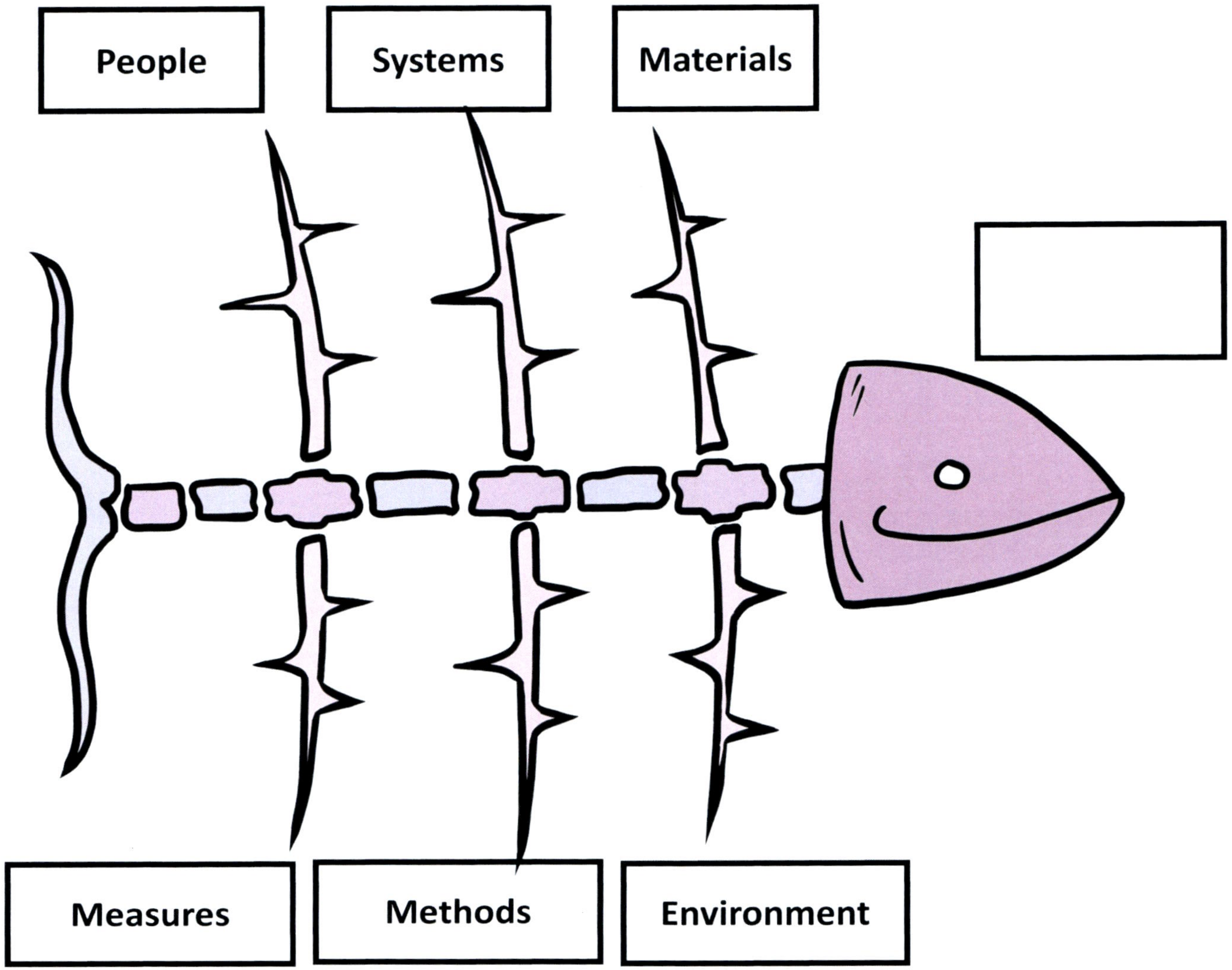

Materials **Systems** **People**

Environment **Methods** **Measures**

Adapted from Figure 4.9 Fishbone analysis

Taken from Chapter 4 – Treating the Root Cause – in "The Effective Team's Operational Excellence Workbook", RiverRhee Publishing, 2015

What might go wrong	Likelihood	Impact	Control measures in place?	LxIxC	Mitigation plans

Adapted from Table 5.3 Failure Mode Effect Analysis

Taken from Chapter 5 – Exploring the Solutions – in "The Effective Team's Operational Excellence Workbook", RiverRhee Publishing, 2015

Further Reading

Bicheno, John. (2004) *The New Lean Toolbox*. PICSIE Books.

Covey, Stephen R. and Whitman, Bob. (2009) *Predictable Results in Unpredictable Times.* Franklin Covey Publishing

George, Michael L. (2003) *Lean Six Sigma for Service*. McGraw-Hill

Goldratt, Eliyahu M. and Cox, Jeff. (2004) *The Goal.* Gower

Goodman, Elisabeth (2012) Information Analysis: a Lean and Six Sigma case study. Business Information Review (29) 83-86

Goodman, Elisabeth C. (2013) *The Effective Team's Change Management Workbook.* RiverRhee Publishing

Hammond, Sue A. (2013) *The Thin Book of Appreciative Inquiry*. Thin Book Publishing

Morgan, John and Brenig-Jones, Martin. (2012) *Lean Six Sigma for Dummies.* John Wiley and Sons

Munro, Roderich A. et al (2008) *The Certified 6 Sigma Green Belt Handbook* . ASQ

Spear, Steven J. (2010) The High-Velocity Edge. McGraw-Hill

The Kaizone (2014) *5 whys folklore. The truth behind a monumental mystery.* http://thekaizone.com/2014/08/5-whys-folklore-the-truth-behind-a-monumental-mystery/ (accessed 4th April 2015)

Womack, James P. and Jones, Daniel T. (2006) *Lean Thinking*. Free Press Business